HAMAN THE MAGNIFICENT. Page 66.

ESTHER AND HER TIMES

IN A SERIES OF

LECTURES

ON THE

BOOK OF ESTHER.

By JOHN M. LOWRIE,
FORT WAYNE, INDIANA.

PHILADELPHIA:
PRESBYTERIAN BOARD OF PUBLICATION,
No. 821 Chestnut Street.

STEREOTYPED BY JESPER HARDING & SON, PHILADELPHIA.

PREFACE.

THE THEME of this volume has been furnished to its writer from so high a source, that modesty does not forbid him to regard the things here treated of, as of the deepest interest and value. That he should rise to the dignity of his subject was not to be expected; to fall far below is not so great a matter, since truth has a value apart from the ability of its advocates, and the most valuable teachings are usually plain and simple. Indeed if it were possible to select a hundred discourses—the best specimens of eloquent, forcible, and instructive preaching in the history of the church—and present them, consecutively, before any people, in a single pulpit, within a year or two, the success of the plan would be small, either to secure interest, or to do good. No element is more important to the interest and profit of any teaching than appropriateness of occasion and place. "A word fitly spoken is like apples of gold in pictures of silver."* The foolishness of preaching is the chosen instrumentality of Divine wisdom for the spread of the gospel; a living

* Prov. xxv. 11.

ministry the church will ever require; and the successful style of preaching in every age will be that which is most nearly adapted to the circumstances and demands of the times. It is no wonder that hundreds of pastors are highly esteemed by their own congregations, not only for their kind sympathies and their wholesome counsels, but also for able and eloquent public ministrations, who yet never acquire an extended reputation. It is no wonder that discourses which have held an audience spell-bound in their delivery, yet do not seem of any special excellence when committed to the printed page. Intellectual power in a pastor is but one of the elements of his usefulness. He should be a "scribe well instructed in the kingdom of righteousness;" but his wisdom is as needful to apply the truth as to expound it. His Lord has described his office as that of a steward, giving to each of his fellow servants "his portion of meat in due season." And no man can be such a steward; no man can enter into the feelings of others so as to reach their necessities, without awakening his own affections and sympathies to such a degree as to shape his meditations, chasten his delivery, and modulate his tones to suit the various exigencies of his people. Hence there is an impropriety in applying to the usual discourses of the pulpit, the rules of rhetorical composition or logical discussion, which may justly apply to the occasional efforts of elaborate oratory. Many a useful and excellent sermon owes its chief attraction to paragraphs of local interest; to allusions understood only by the hearers; or to the greater stress laid upon certain points which a logical treatment of the topic would have placed in a minor position. It strengthens these thoughts to notice that the most famous discourses in all ages have been called forth by special occasions; and that the best remains of many a public speaker are not those upon which he has bestowed the greatest thought and care.

But though the fitting word to the occasion is so important to the interest and profit of public instructions, we may not therefore argue that every preacher should confine his teachings to his immediate hearers; that printed discourses are unprofitable; or that a reader may not, in some degree, sympathize with the original circumstances that are involved in the speaker's words. We contend that no book can displace the living teacher of the gospel; but we claim that much pleasure and profit may be derived from the publication of discourses that have been preached before a congregation, and that bear the marks of adaptation to their particular occasions. There are even advantages which the reader has, especially in a series of discourses, over those that have heard them. If he is willing to make allowances for the feebler passages, that are necessary to maintain the connection; for the occasional introduction and urgency of thoughts, that appear to him little relevant; for repetitions, that may be natural and proper in discourses separated in their delivery by weeks and months; and for the diffuseness of style, that suits the pulpit better than the volume, the reader can better get the impression of the whole; better select his own favourable time for the lessons afforded him; and better ponder the more forcible thoughts that seem to require more than a single hearing.

The writer of these pages, as a pastor, is constantly accustomed to lecture upon the Scenes and Characters of the Bible. He regards this as the Scriptural mode of presenting truth; for the Sacred Volume is our first and chief model for that interesting style of picture-writing, now so generally adopted by our best historians, biographers, and even essayists. Even before he entered the sacred ministry, his attention was called to the Book of Esther by a volume of Lectures upon it by the Rev. Dr. Thomas McCrie; and to this unpretending little volume alone—one of surpassing interest—does he feel under obligations demanding special acknowledgment, for the thoughts and conduct of these discourses.

Convinced that the Book of Esther is too little known even to serious readers of the Bible; persuaded that those whose minds are fairly awakened to it, will ever afterwards regard it as one of the most interesting portions of the word of God; and hoping that these Lectures may serve to call the attention of some to this portion of the inspired pages, to impart interest to many of the incidents which a casual reader might deem of little importance, and thus to enforce the lessons of inspired wisdom after this volume itself has been laid aside; he would lay this publication within the reach of christian readers. In the whole matter, he is less desirous, he trusts, of public favour, than of the Divine smile upon an humble attempt to glorify HIS WORD, HIS GRACE, HIS PROVIDENCE, AND HIMSELF.

CONTENTS.

LECTURE III.

HAMAN, THE MAGNIFICENT.

LECTURE IV.

THE IRREVERSIBLE DECREE.

LECTURE V.

DIVINE DESIGNS AND HUMAN DUTY.

LECTURE VI.

ESTHER'S NOBLE RESOLVE.

LECTURE VII.

THE SLEEPLESS NIGHT.

LECTURE VIII.

THE EXALTATION OF MORDECAI.

LECTURE IX.

THE FALL OF HAMAN.

PAGE

LECTURE X.

THE DECREE REVERSED.

LECTURE XI.

THE DAY OF CONFLICT.

LECTURE XII.

THE FEAST PURIM.

ESTHER AND HER TIMES.

LECTURE I.

THE DIVORCE OF VASHTI.

The Book of Esther is one of unknown authorship among the tracts composing the sacred volume. Even the age, to which we are to refer the events here recorded, cannot be unquestionably determined. We may believe that it was written by the man who here bears the name of Mordecai; and even if we are mistaken in this conjecture, it is a matter of little importance. For the argument to sustain the authenticity of any portion of the sacred volume, may be independent of the writer's name, except when that name is expressly given; and there are several books in the Bible whose authors' names are not given in the books themselves. It is sufficient to name Judges, Kings, Chronicles, and the Epistle to the Hebrews.

The position of this book in the sacred canon and its inspired authority have sometimes been questioned, but we think without good reason. Its name is omitted in some of the catalogues, made by the early fathers, of the sacred books; and it is a very common and certainly a very striking objection to a book claiming inspired authority, that in the genuine and Hebrew chapters of the Book of Esther, the name of God is not mentioned from one end to the other. But these objections, merely negative in themselves, are of small weight against the more numerous and sterling proofs, which establish its right to a place in the sacred volume. The Book of Esther is contained in the Hebrew Bibles; it has ever been received by the Jews; and as it was beyond question contained in their canon when our Lord Jesus Christ was upon earth; and as, though he charged them with corrupt doctrines, he never charged them with corrupting the Scriptures themselves, we may justly argue that he set the seal of his approval upon the Scriptures as they possessed them. This he did without qualification or exception. (See John v. 39.) Besides, the later Jews regard the Book of Esther as ranking in veneration next to the Pentateuch; they yet observe with peculiar interest the feast of Purim, of which mention is made in this book alone, and which was established to commemorate the deliverance that this book records; and this feast affords strong confirmatory proof of the history here given. To all which we may add, that though a few of the earlier catalogues omit the name of this book, it was generally received; it is mentioned in the catalogues of

Jerome, Augustine, the Third Council of Carthage Canon XLVII, and the Council of Laodicea Canon LX: and the striking and oft repeated remark of the pious Matthew Henry is well worthy of being remembered, "If the *name* of God is not in it, his *finger* is."

There are nearly seven chapters added to this book in the Latin Vulgate and in the English Douay version as used by the Church of Rome; but, for good and valid reasons, they are esteemed apocryphal, and of no authority whatever. In his edition of the Vulgate, Jerome expressly notes where these begin; and declares truly that they are not found in the Hebrew at all. This is acknowledged in the margin of the Douay; while it is there added, without the slightest foundation, "that the Seventy-two Interpreters translated them out of the Hebrew, or added them by inspiration of the Holy Ghost." The doubtfulness of tone used in the very assertion furnishes its sufficient answer, and proves it to be a mere conjecture. In the absence of all proof of the authenticity of these chapters, we may easily sum up these valid reasons for their rejection. They are not found in the Hebrew; the Jews have never received them; they not only differ in style and sentiment from the earlier chapters, but they are greatly inferior; the very first spurious verse mentions the name of God, and these chapters often repeat it—in striking contrast with the chapters in the Hebrew, where, as already noticed, this name never occurs; and these additional chapters abound in errors, and even in statements which contradict the genuine portion of the book. These apocryphal chapters make Mordecai a great man before he detected the conspiracy against the king: and they place this conspiracy before the repudiation of one queen, and the marriage of the other; both which matters are contradictory to the genuine book of Esther. Moreover Haman is here called a Macedonian, though previously an Agagite. These difficulties sufficiently warrant the rejection of chapters, which have no plausible claims to prefer for their inspired authority.

The TIME when these events occurred can as little be accurately determined. We judge it is evidently not before the return of the Jewish people from the Babylonish captivity. The royal city, according to this narrative, is SHUSHAN. This determines that the monarch was not a Median, but a Persian; and refers the history to a period subsequent to Darius the Mede. Happily the instructive character of the book is not affected by the discordant answers to the inquiry, Who was this Ahasuerus? Darius Hystaspis, Xerxes, Artaxerxes Longimanus, and Ochus have been variously conjectured.

We suppose we are not far from the proper period of history, and as likely correct as otherwise in the man, if we adopt Artaxerxes Longimanus, the son of Xerxes, as the Ahasuerus of this book. It is an interesting coincidence, and we judge one corroborative of our correctness in this, that to regard this as the period will connect the elevation of Esther, not only with this recorded deliverance of her people, but with the favour shown by a Persian king to Ezra and Nehemiah, that they might rebuild Jerusalem. Nothing is more natural than to see this king protect and strengthen the Jews, sending them back to their own land, and assisting to rebuild their ancient temple, if in the Providence of their God, he had married a Jewish maiden.

That there should be no certainty in reference to persons and dates, as connected with this book, is matter of small surprise to a reflecting mind. It is very little that the most learned men know concerning ages so remote in the history of the world; the Bible itself is our most reliable source of information; and this sacred volume was not designed to furnish us with the annals of the pagan nations. Although the book of Esther is among the last of the historical writings of the Old Testament, it is well for us to remember that the earliest writings of profane history date back only thus far. Herodotus, though usually called the Father of History, began to write about the same time that the books of Ezra and Nehemiah were composed: and these, at the latest, are not more than contemporaneous with the book of Esther. The writings of Moses are the plainest and most consistent of ancient history; and they are almost alone in referring to these periods of remote antiquity. In the inspired volume, God has given to the world the genealogy of the race as it is nowhere else to be found; and though the darkness of human history often serves as a hiding place for the sceptic and the scoffer, yet the diversities of those that impugn the sacred narratives, their endless subterfuges, and their contradictions of each other, from one age to another, are important proofs of error ; and in these things, they stand in remarkable contrast with the dignity and simplicity and harmony of the inspired writers. And we may notice also, that when the line of sacred historians stops, though from this period profane records begin, there is, at these remote ages, much confusion in human history; the dates are often unsettled, and the important characters are often poorly described.

Scarcely any book in the Bible has a more definite aim or a plainer lesson in its history than the book of Esther. Its simple object is to exhibit the workings of God's providence at a remarkable crisis, for the deliverance of his people. This is effected in the use of natural means, and by the instrumentality of both good and bad men ; and yet in such a way, that the finger of God is evidently seen, even in those minute and separated particulars which, when they occur, seem of trifling significance and without connection.

It would seem proper for us, in this opening Lecture, to consider the condition of the Jews in the dispersion, for whom this deliverance was wrought;

and the reasons for the Divine forbearance towards that portion of the Jews who still remained in the lands of their dispersion. After this, we will notice the first step preparatory to the great deliverance: the divorce of Vashti as the queen of Persia.

The destruction of the Jewish State, and the captivity of that people in the Babylonish Empire, was the just judgment of their covenant God upon them, for long continued national sins. This captivity lasted through seventy years; and the return was regarded as the dawning of the Divine favour upon the chastened people. But it is an inquiry of some interest, How would God deal with that portion of the nation, that refused or neglected to return from Babylon? We might hastily judge that those, who had too little love for the Holy Land, and too little zeal for the rebuilding of the temple, to induce them to leave the lands of paganism, had forfeited the favour of Jehovah; and that he would work no wonders on their behalf. But upon a closer view, we need have no surprise that God's providence still specially regards the scattered Jews; and that this book records his mercy to those that were still in exile. The people were urged to go up, by their inspired prophets; it was highly important that the city and the temple should be rebuilt. It may have been gross failure in duty in many a Jew that he chose still to abide in the land of the captivity; and yet is it no marvel of God's providence, that he watched over those that remained, and blessed them still in their exile.

We may consider in reference to this matter :

1st. That God graciously condescends to meet man upon the low grounds where he stands, and to grant his favours even though we are undeserving of them. We must ever acknowledge, "He hath not dealt with us after our sins, nor rewarded us according to our iniquities." The differences between the people of God on earth are not such as to allow any to boast of duty performed, in a manner so exemplary as to merit the Divine favour. There are infirmities in all; and the grace of God is continually manifested towards the undeserving. No man indeed can be right who justifies his sin or neglect of duty, on the plea that God is merciful; and that is a plain dictate of inspiration, "If I regard iniquity in my heart, the Lord will not hear me." God sees and frowns upon sin in any man; he withholds the smile of his regard from his backsliding children; he sends his word to convince them of their folly, and his judgments to chastise them for it; and perhaps, according to the records of this history, he awakened the attention of the Jews in Persia by these events of terror and dismay, which yet issued in a deliverance so marked and glorious. Had they not been a sinning people, they might not have been exposed to the arts of wicked Haman, if they had not been God's covenant people, they would not have been delivered from his power.

The Lord does not smile upon sin; but when his people are negligent of duty, he chastises them. Still he does not forsake them. If even we decide that the Jews remaining in the exile were unmindful of their duty, we can easily reconcile it with Jehovah's holiness and faithfulness, that he watched over them in mercy.

We may consider,

2nd. That there were some obvious reasons to extenuate, and even to justify the apparent disobedience of many of those, who yet did not return to the Holy Land at the bidding of the prophets. We might suppose that if the piety of the entire people had been ardent and zealous; if they had all grieved at the waters of Babylon, like the prophet who hanged his "harp upon the willows," and preferred Jerusalem above his chief joy, Ps. cxxxvii. 2; if they had taken "pleasure in the stones" and favoured "the dust" of Zion, Ps. cii. 14; they would have received with gladness the long desired permission to return from the land of the stranger. But let us not forget the real difficulties of the case. At the bidding of their own prophets, the Jews in the captivity had bought lands and built houses in these foreign countries; they had been industrious and submissive subjects; they had identified their own interests with the prosperity of the government, Jer. xxix. 4—7; some of their own most eminent men had been high in office and enjoyed the favour of their monarchs, Neh. i. 11; and as the natural result of all these things, strong attachments had been formed by property, and by friendship, and in many cases, doubtless, by marked usefulness to the gentile population around them. That they had seldom been persecuted, and that such men as Daniel and Nehemiah had enjoyed influence and distinction, would tend greatly to strengthen their ties of attachment to a foreign soil. Let us not fail also to remember the length of the exile. After their stay in Babylon and its provinces had been prolonged to seventy years, it is obvious that very few of the people could have any remembrance at all of Judea, or any personal attachments urging their return there. It was still indeed the land of their fathers; that soil was included in the covenant made with Abraham; there the Messiah was to appear, and all their fond religious associations gathered around the Holy Land. Not only their sacred books told them of God's promises; not only their prophets urged their return, when the set time had come; but their aged men recounted in their ears their early recollections of that splendid temple, which had been, in its day, the only spot specially consecrated to Jehovah's worship in the world which he had made. But the vast majority of the people—we may well say the entire body of the active population—were natives of Babylon; the original captives were chiefly dead and laid in foreign graves; and to remove this population back to Judea was no easy task. Take any people, and place them and their children for seventy years in another land, constantly forming their attachments there, and their entire removal will prove impracticable. The cases are not fully analogous; but every man can realize how impossible it would be, to send back to Europe, the people and their descendants, who have settled in America and remained on the western continent for the space of seventy years.

Besides the difficulties thus suggested against the return of the entire people, or even the great mass of them, from Babylon to Judea, other difficulties also can easily be understood. Many may have desired to return who were not free to carry out their own wishes. We cannot reasonably suppose that every Jew was truly pious; and the ungodly portion of the people would care as little to leave their comfortable abodes and return to Judea, as the ungodly portion of our population cares to part with their property for the spread and support of Christian missions. Through the influence of these, many pious persons of a better disposition, may have remained in the dispersion. Many a pious wife or child may have been kept away from Judea by a careless husband or father: and many a Jewish servant of a heathen master may have been unable to leave his place of servitude.

We have at least one example of the detention in the land of the captivity against his desire, of one who was both a pious man and a prophet. Nehemiah was cup-bearer to the king; and while his heart was with his distant brethren, his services were demanded in the palace. The king held him in high estimation, and when he saw his sad countenance, and knew the cause, he allowed him to go to the aid of his brethren. But even then he set a time for his absence, and exacted of him a pledge of return. His case seems to prove that many Jews remained in the land of their exile, who would gladly have gone to Jerusalem.

But this matter is farther explained in an interesting record found in the prophetical writings of Zechariah. During the building of the second temple, the people who returned to Jerusalem were poor; and having all the disadvantages of a long emigration, and building up anew the desolated city, they found their resources inadequate to restore that costly temple. In these circumstances, the superior wealth of their brethren, who remained in the dispersion, was of essential advantage for the progress of a work that was of common interest. And these brethren were not unmindful of their share in Jerusalem's temple. Perhaps they did not even wait for solicitations to contribute. So, according to the record in Zechariah, a deputation was at one time sent to Jerusalem, consisting of Heldai, Tobijah, and Jedaiah, who brought gold and silver for the building of the temple. At this time the question was definitely settled by Divine authority, that the Jews, who did not come to Jerusalem, should yet have part in the temple which they had thus assisted to erect.

The prophet, who records the transaction, was commanded to take a portion of their gold and silver, and make crowns,—a single crown of several circlets,—to place this symbolically upon the head of the High Priest; and then to lay it up in the temple for a memorial that these deputies and their brethren who sent them with their gift, had a part in the building and in the blessings of the Lord's house. Thus the Lord declared that the Jews afar off, as well as the Jews near, should build in the temple; giving proof that many accepted people were yet in the captivity; giving full recognition of their interest in the covenant of Abraham; and giving a prophetic pledge of the gathering of more distant ones—even the scattered gentiles—unto the greater temple of which this was but a type, and whose Builder should be THE BRANCH OF THE LORD, the great Messiah himself! See Zech. vi. 9—15.

These thoughts will assist us to form a just opinion of the condition of the Jews who yet remained in the lands of exile. Some were ungodly doubtless, and careless of their high birthright as the sons of Israel; some, had their piety been deeper, would have returned to the land of promise: and many, far from the beloved temple and the dwelling place of the covenant, maintained a holy and consistent life; loved the ordinances of God; worshipped, like Daniel, with their faces towards the holy city; and by faith, in remembrance of the morning and evening altar in distant Judea, hoped for the Divine acceptance. Over such a people God's holy providence watched.

But 3d, it is worthy of our notice especially that God had designs to serve of a most important nature, by the detention of so large a portion of the Jewish people in the realm of Persia, and by their still wider dispersion in all the earth. His providential designs do not form indeed the just rule of man's duty; the Jews may have been wrong in not returning, though God might overrule even their sin for good. We are to judge of man's sinfulness by principles, not by Providence; by his departure from commanded duty, not by the results which God may work. We may see in this interesting portion of the history of the church, that God overruled for good, not only the Babylonish captivity itself, which was a punishment upon the Jews for national sins; but also the fact that so many, perhaps often wrongfully, remained in the dispersion. God's great design in human history was, first, to send his Son as a Mediator and Redeemer: and next, through him to preach the gospel to every creature. The first generations of men "did not like to retain God in their knowledge," Rom. i. 21, 28; and he gave the earth up to blindness of mind and ignorance of salvation. But to save the principles of true religion from perishing, he called Abraham, and in his family established the Jewish church, and built around it walls of exclusive and separated interests, conservative of the great principles of piety, until the rest of the world had tried man's own awful experiment, and found how little man's wisdom can know of God without a Revealer. 1 Cor. i. 21. But as the fulness of time drew on, and the long promised Messiah was about to come, it was needful that the way should be prepared, both in the world and in this exclusive church. The prejudices of the Jews were to be removed; their national pride was to be humbled; the cherished services of their peculiar economy were to be made oppressive and burdensome, on the one hand; while some knowledge of the true religion was to be extended to the Gentiles; their expectations were to be awakened for the coming of a great Prince; their languages were to be acquired, and a footing obtained in their different kingdoms, on the other hand; and all this as preparatory to teaching all nations, and setting up the universal kingdom of Christ. How comprehensive the Divine plan! How simple the means to secure these great purposes! To humble Jewish pride and to destroy the influence of the Levitical system, their magnificent temple was burned to ashes; its peculiar contents were lost beyond the possibility of recovery; the ark of the covenant, with its precious accompaniments, the two tables of stone, the Shekinah, the rod of Aaron, and the pot of incorruptible manna, perished; even their sacred language was so lost that after their return, when Ezra read the law of the Lord at Jerusalem in the original Hebrew, he was obliged to "give the sense and cause the people to understand the meaning." Nehem. viii. 8. To subdue their prejudices, and indeed to render it impossible to keep the ceremonial law, the people were exiled from Judea. For more than seventy years, they had neither temple nor altar; and even after the rebuilding of the temple, it was quite impracticable for the scattered Jews to assemble three times a year at Jerusalem as their law required. To keep the law was impossible; and, perhaps to their surprise, their covenant God continued his mercies when the law was not kept. Thus they were gradually led to see the difficulties of their law, and prepared for a system which would abrogate it. So one Jew declares that it was a burden "that neither we nor our fathers were able to bear;" Acts xv. 10; and another that it had "decayed and waxed old and was ready to vanish away." Heb. viii. 13.

But it is of very great interest for us to notice the design of God's providence for preaching the gospel in all the world, and for establishing Christ's universal kingdom, by means of the Jewish dispersion. The scattered Jews were God's prepared missionaries; as possibly it may yet be found that the dispersed seed even now shall again be made in all lands the chief chosen heralds of the latter day glory, when the "veil shall be removed" from their faces; 2 Cor. iii. 16; and their receiving shall be "like life from the dead" to the gentile world. Rom. xi. 12, 15. We are told that upon the day of Pentecost, the Spirit poured out upon the apostles, im parted miraculously the ability to speak in foreign languages; but that miracle did not need frequent repetition for the wide spread of the gospel. God's providence, by natural means, not less remarkable than a miracle, had, during the five hundred years that preceded Christ's coming, provided for the wide spread of the gospel. In this interval between the Babylonish captivity and the death of Christ, the foreign Jews had become more and more widely scattered; and yet retaining the knowledge and the worship of the true God, had their residences in every land and spoke every language. Jerusalem and its temple was the ecclesiastical metropolis of these widely scattered Jews; their chief priests and rulers dwelt in Judea; and they ever kept themselves distinct from the nations around. Thus we find that, on the day of Pentecost, there were dwelling at Jerusalem, "Jews, devout men out of every nation under heaven." Acts ii. 5. These men were well qualified to judge of the genuineness of the miracle of speaking with tongues; and among the thousands then converted to God were many fully qualified, without such a miracle, to spread the gospel abroad. Already they spoke, as their vernacular, the languages of all the world. These men became missionaries, not by going among strangers and picking up a meagre acquaintance with the language and modes of thought of a strange people; but by going home to the neighbourhoods where they were born, where they were well known to the people, and where their personal influence was already established; and with the new and strange tidings upon their lips of Christ's death and the Spirit's mission; with a new mind in them; and a new love for souls urging them on, they preached the gospel. We have no detailed account of their preaching; but we know that the triumphs of the gospel were marvellous in that age, and that soon Christianity overthrew the paganism of the Roman empire. A just view of the revolutions of Christianity is a wide view. The providence of God had been preparing for these triumphs for centuries. The fulness of time had come when the Son of God appeared. Gal. iv. 4.

These thoughts explain the dispersion of the Jews, and their detention in the lands of exile; and they vindicate the Divine protection of the scattered people. Evil threatens them indeed. God could have prevented the schemes of Haman, or his rise to power. But it is not by keeping his people from trial, that he tests their graces, exhibits his mercy, or awakens their gratitude. He leads us through temptations to show our faith, and to give experience of his faithfulness. We shall see, as we proceed, that the wicked designs of an enemy to the church, do but set forth more gloriously God's providence for Zion. We shall see God the same to his people in all ages; and in the church the same essential doctrines, the same substantial duties, the same salutary fears, the same exercise of faith, the same covenanted safety.

But before closing the present lecture, we proposed to notice the first step in readiness for the great deliverance. This is the divorce of the haughty Vashti, preparatory to the elevation of a Jewish maiden to the throne of Persia.

The evil against which God's providence prepares is not yet apparent to the eye of man; indeed the plot of mischief has not as yet been conceived in the mind of the Agagite, the chief mover in it. What a comfortable reflection to the people of God is this, that even before the sky is overcast by the dark clouds of a threatening storm, there is a mind acquainted with all the hidden future, that even now prepares a deliverance from the unforeseen evil! We know not why God makes such changes in our lot; but all the changes around us may be directly in preparation for some great event, involving our comfort or safety. Even the doings of folly and the crimes of injustice are under his control, to subserve his purposes of truth and righteousness. Men may form their plans, and form them in iniquity; they may trample upon every sacred right of others, and every duty in themselves; and they may seem to prosper. Yet God brings to pass his purposes of judgment to sinners and good to the righteous; the hour when the wicked seem nearest to triumph is often just before their irrecoverable fall; and the very means relied upon for success often become the instruments of their failure.

> "There is a power
> Unseen, that rules the illimitable world;
> That guides its motions from the brightest star
> To the least dust of this sin-tainted world:
> While man, who madly deems himself the lord
> Of all, is nought but weakness and dependence."

Behold now the great Ahasuerus and the splendour of his festival in the palace at Shushan! "He reigned from India to Ethiopia, over one hundred and twenty-seven provinces." What a lamentable thought that one man should have control, so complete and arbitrary, over so many myriads of his fellow men! How impossible was it for him, with all the diligence of the busiest life, and all the wisdom of the finest intellect, and all the indomitable energy of an earnest responsibility, to rule in so vast an empire, so as to secure the real good of his subjects! To a man who comprehends their weight, and is at all disposed to attempt the duties they bring, the cares of a great government are no object of envy. But what are the employments of this great king as we are here introduced to him? Such, alas! as king's palaces often show; neither augmenting the royal dignity, nor preparing for royal duties. Is this the glory of a kingdom? A feast of wine, a drunken monarch, an unjust divorce!

Shall we stay to notice this gorgeous feast, according to the state of the king? The splendid hangings of the halls, the couches covered with cloth of gold and silver, the floor of tesselated marble, are even exceeded in magnificence by the drinking cups. It was reckoned disgraceful among the Persians to use vessels of earth. These were of gold, and diverse one from another: *i. e.*, as some suppose, the same cup not used twice during six months' feasting. Perhaps rather, each cup of a different pattern. The engraving upon a golden cup might be far more valuable than the material.

We will not stay to mourn over a people whose rulers could afford to spend six months in such frivolous engagements, and neglect the duties of government. Indeed the gay luxury and idleness of Artaxerxes were a blessing to Persia, compared with his father's activity; and there is less folly in the drunken revel of Shushan than in the man, who became angry at the waves of the sea, and scourged and chained the Hellespont! Yet here are two matters of Persian propriety in their feasts. The queen and her women held their feast apart, and in the king's palace no man was compelled to drink beyond his own choice. Many a man in Christian lands would have been saved from a drunkard's grave, had not scoffing companions and a perverted public opinion forced upon him the fatal cup, which he would not have tasted if none did compel. The pagan king gives orders that every man may act his own pleasure, but inexorable and more arbitrary custom in Christian lands exceeds in cruel tyranny.

Happily the usages of society are better in this matter than they were; but we fear to say that men are safe even now, where the wine cup sparkles.

Six months of feasting have passed—another week has been added; and the last day of so protracted a festival is the most important of all. But for the king's concluding folly the world would never have heard of this gay feasting. A drunken man is ready for any folly; and a drunken king differs from a drunken beggar, only because he can command the execution of his maudlin schemes, and lift his shame into greater mischief and greater notoriety. The most sacred things are base in the eyes of such a man; and the sweet proprieties of life are in danger of the grossest violation. An intoxicated man often displays his ruling passions in an indecorous manner. King Ahasuerus was proud of his queen's beauty. And now, forgetful of those Persian customs, which forbade the public appearance of females, and of his own duty as a husband, he gave orders that the beautiful Vashti should leave her own apartments in the palace, and appear before the impudent gaze of his drunken princes. This order was equally dishonourable to the king who uttered it, and to the queen who heard it. A man never more disgraces himself than when he puts an affront upon his own wife.

But if the husband is drunk, the wife is sober. Queen Vashti refused to come. We may blame or approve her conduct, as we attribute it to pride, or to virtue. If her public appearance at her husband's command was such a violation of Persian ideas as to subject her to the charge of immodest behaviour, she did right to refuse. No father has a right to demand of his daughter, no husband has a right to command in his wife, any departure from modesty or virtue. It is possible, however, that the queen refused through pride. The command was perhaps imprudent; but not reckoned immodest. In that case her reluctant and modest appearance, through respect to her husband, would have been right; every sensible mind would make allowance for her circumstances; and her modesty would have suffered nothing from the discharge of an unpleasant duty.

The astounding announcement is made in the royal presence—The queen will not come. Flushed with wine, the king was exceedingly angry, and the presence of his lords yet more irritated him. Upon consultation with the wise men, it was immediately resolved, not that the queen should be put to death, but that a public example should be made of her,—that she should be degraded from her place as queen, and divorced as a wife. No time is taken for proper deliberation; no space is left for a change of purpose; the counsellors yet feel the influence of the wine cup, when the unalterable decree is passed. It is some advantage that counsel was taken, and that the divorce of Vashti was pronounced according to law. For now no blood is shed, even in the wrath of the king. The design of Providence is quietly reached. The queenly throne of Persia is vacated; the first step is taken for the great end which this book commemorates; room is prepared for the ascent of an humble Jewish maiden to the highest earthly dignity; all things move forward to deliver the chosen people of God.

We may close this lecture with these brief reflections.

How perishing and unsatisfactory and unprofitable are the engagements and pleasures of worldly men! In the highest ranks of life, with all that can minister to pride or luxury, they are no objects of envy. We see here the pomp and splendour of one of earth's mightiest kings; and perhaps no earthly records make mention of a more sumptuous banquet than this of Ahasuerus. But six months of revelry soon passed; and though such pernicious extravagance may have oppressed his subjects, and the report have astonished them, we are even indebted for the knowledge that such a feast was ever held, to a history that Persians did not write, and in which the mighty king of one hundred and twenty-seven provinces plays quite a subordinate part. We may well hold in light esteem the revelries and luxuries of a perishable world. Little worthy of our envy or our imitation is the earthly course of men who say, "Let us eat and drink, for to-morrow we die." "Let us crown ourselves with rose-buds before they are withered." "The fashion of this world," in its best estate, "passes away." They only are happy whose names and deeds and characters are associated with the covenant people of God. Over them God exercises his special care; their names are written in imperishable annals, and their portion is a satisfactory and an abiding one. Kings, like Ahasuerus, may feast and die and be forgotten: queens, like Vashti, may indulge their pride and fall from their thrones into oblivion; but the humblest of God's people, sometimes drawn forth from obscurity to places of honour, sometimes left unknown to the world, shall be noticed by his eye, preserved by his kind providence, and blessed with his favour. No wisdom is worthy of the name, but true piety; no ambition can reward our care, but that which aspires to be accepted of God; no pleasures are lasting, but the enjoyments we find in serving him. What is earth with the power and splendour of Ahasuerus—with all the queenly dignity and womanly beauty of Vashti? "What is a man profited if he gain the whole world and lose his own soul?" This most momentous of earthly questions it well becomes us to ponder.

LECTURE II.

MORDECAI RAISED UP.

THE divorce of Vashti was pronounced after a consultation with legal counsellors, and ratified by the forms of legal authority. But what an evidence have we of legislative folly, not in a single man, but in an entire race of Persian kings, that so absurd a law should control the Empire! The laws of the Medes and Persians were unalterable. If we were speaking of the laws of an infinite and unchanging God; if we consider that no unforeseen contingencies can arise in his government; that his laws, devised in infinite knowledge, wisdom, and justice, cannot be altered for the better; and that his own excellence forbids any decline from their perfection;—if we were speaking of such a ruler, and of his laws, we might wisely affirm that they change not. But in human lawgivers, or in human executives—whether of church or state—the claim of infallibility may excite our contempt. Ignorant, foolish, full of prejudice, and liable to error from a thousand causes, man should lay no claim to unswerving correctness in forming his judgments, or in framing his laws; and an unjust and oppressive law incapable of repeal becomes the instrument of more pernicious tyranny. Continual changing in human laws is an evil oppressive upon the people; but scarcely any abuse of the power to alter the laws can be worse than the inability, in shortsighted and erring men, to change at all.

It is possible that the king repented of his haste in divorcing his lovely queen. The act of a moment, when wine had clouded his reason and inflamed his anger, and when he himself had provoked her act of insubordination, was one which cooler moments, and the sweet memories of former affection, might wish to recall. But the monarch is himself bound by that foolish law; and the act of an intoxicated council is as permanent as the wisest and most deliberate legislation. The true law of marriage, as ordained by Jehovah, would have forbidden a divorce for any such occasion as the Persian queen had afforded, even taking her offence in its most aggravated form; but the foolish lusts of man had long since trampled under foot and forgotten the ordinances of that eternal King, whose laws need no improvement. It is not needful for us to say, that the entire plan adopted for securing a successor to Vashti, was a transgression of the divine laws respecting marriage. The Bible is remarkable for this; that very often its historians give us the simple narrative of transactions, and make few remarks to approve or condemn conduct the most meritorious or the most iniquitous. So is it here. The plan adopted by the king is explained; we are thus told the cruel and arbitrary customs of other lands and ages; yet it is by our own comparisons of these facts with the principles taught in the Scriptures, that we learn how different all this is from the law of God. And as we gratefully see how different is the state of social manners among us, let us acknowledge that the difference is owing to the influence of the Bible and Christianity. Marriage with us is founded upon no caprice of a despot, but upon the mutual affection and consent of the parties; it is followed by no such desolation and cruel desertion, worse than widowhood, as falls upon the crowd of imprisoned and neglected females in an eastern seraglio; it secures the mutual happiness of two individuals; and demands, if the wife shall give up all others for her husband alone, so the husband shall give up all others solely for his wife. For thus was it from the beginning. God made one man and one woman. And this is the true exhibition of "women's rights;" the right to occupy a sphere, appropriate and divinely appointed: a sphere as to bustle and display and vain glory inferior to that of man; as to dignity not his equal; but a sphere as to virtue and happiness and usefulness often quite equal, often quite superior to that of man.

No solution is even given in the narrative of the fact that a Jewish maiden consents to share an arrangement that would make her the bride of a heathen prince; and even Mordecai seems to make no effort to secure her exemption. Marriages with the heathen were a forbidden thing to the Jews; and we would suppose that persons of so much piety as Esther and Mordecai, would dread her alliance even with the king. That they were now exiles in a foreign land would expose them more to such alliances; but the true influence of such liability should have been to place them more upon their guard. Yet we may solve the matter consistently with their piety and with all due modesty in Esther. The wishes of females are usually but little consulted in eastern marriages; but especially when arrangements are made for a king's marriage, a family of Jewish captives could not have resisted his will. If the fame of the beautiful Esther had spread through her own neighbourhood; if in this inquiry for fair young ladies, her name had been breathed to the king's officers, neither she nor Mordecai could have resisted the royal mandate. Force they could not use; concealment would avail but little; and entreaties would have been derided by men in whose eyes it was only too great an honour that the Jewish maiden should find even the meanest place in the harem of the great Ahasuerus. Besides, Mordecai had every confidence in the wisdom and goodness of God's wonder-working providence. This place for Esther had been none of his seeking or hers. The change in the king's household that had led to this matter, he might regard as providential; and in the deep dependence of his people perhaps he judged that God was preparing some kindness for Israel through the influence of a Jewish queen. It is a lesson of importance in matters of providence, that when God works differently from our purposes and desires, we may wait quietly and hopefully for farther movements from his hand, who often deals with us better than our fears. When changes are wrought in our condition, through our own seeking, and by our own active instrumentality; when voluntarily we have exposed ourselves to temptation, or run into evil, we may not justly charge our troubles to the orderings of Providence, or feel that they are any thing else than the natural results of our own folly and sin. But when honours come unsought; and dangers appear in a path where God has led; we may take even trouble as designed only to try our faith; and we may rely confidently upon the guidance and protection of a faithful God. Esther entered the palace of Ahasuerus, all unknowing of that career of honour to which her God was guiding her.

If Esther's selection at such a time is evidence of her beauty, it is pleasing to notice farther proof of her prudence. She made no extravagant demands of the officer to whom she and her companions were given in charge, and by her modest behaviour she won his esteem and secured his good offices. It is a great pity when beauty is spoiled by petulance and indiscretion, and it greatly heightens the bloom of a fair cheek, when sweet tempered affability is seen in every dimpled smile. In the house of her cousin, Mordecai, she had learned to obey his wishes, and though not comprehending the reason of his request, she did not reveal the nation to which she belonged.

The first twelve months of this new life, before Esther saw the king's face at all, were doubtless long and anxious to her and to Mordecai. Solicitous for his beloved ward, and desirous of knowing that she was well, Mordecai was constant in his attentions upon her, as far as the arrangements of the king's palace would allow. Cruel and irksome indeed were the social arrangements which could separate a maiden like Esther from the visits and the affection of one who had loved her in her orphanage, who had nurtured her in his own abode with all the affection of a father. If he had been her father, there would have been the same cruel separation; and she who had not yet seen her husband, as a new object of affection, is thus secluded from all she had ever loved before. Long hours of dreary loneliness made up that first year; and Mordecai walked every day before the court, perhaps in communication with some of the inmates, to learn what had become of Esther.

We delay no longer to lament the fate of the rejected candidates in this lottery matrimonial. Doubtless, careless lookers-on here might say that the success of this or that damsel was a chance depending partly upon her own beauty, but chiefly upon the caprice or the humour of the king. But chance is an idea that belongs not to the believer's creed. We regard as sinful all dealings in lottery schemes and games of hazard, not only for their mischievous tendencies, but because they imply an unwarranted appeal to the providence of God. Men have no right to call lightly or profanely for Divine interference, or to expect him to settle the stakes of the lottery, the dice-box, or the gaming-table. Strictly speaking there is no chance. God rules over everything. The flight of a sparrow, the fall of a hair, the upturning of a die, the drawing forth of this number or that, he regulates. "The lot is cast into the lap, but the whole disposing thereof is of the Lord." Prov. xvi. 33. When the damsels appear in their succession before the king, God has already chosen the successor of Vashti, and the king's heart is in his hand to turn it where he will. Let men discuss, if they please, the difficulty of recognizing the free agency of man, while yet we acknowledge the efficient providence of God. But the practical truth is plain enough. Man is a free agent, knows that he is, and acts accordingly; but higher than man, GOD TOO IS FREE, does his pleasure, and yet interferes not with man's free action. At Esther's turn to go in she struck all beholders with admiration—she won the king's heart. This is the lower link in the providential chain. But there is a higher and nobler efficacy we must not overlook. IT PLEASED GOD that the Jewish maiden should be queen of Persia.

But it will be proper for us now to turn and consider another character in these interesting scenes, whose name has already occurred, and who bears a conspicuous part in the succeeding transactions. The cousin and protector of Esther was Mordecai, the Jew. The account given of his kindred is clear; but the date of his birth is remarkably ambiguous; and it imparts its ambiguity of date to the entire book of Esther. The record is, "Mordecai, the son of Jair, the son of Shimei, the son of Kish, a Benjamite; who had been carried away from Jerusalem with the captivity which had been carried away with Jeconiah king of Judah, whom Nebuchadnezzar the king of Babylon had carried away." Esth. ii. 5, 6. This is very precise and explicit, except in one thing: we cannot decide who was carried away. Was it Mordecai himself? If so, he was born in Judea; and we must make the date of the book earlier than the end of the seventy years' captivity, or regard him as a very old man in these events. But the passage may mean that Kish was carried captive, and his great grandson, Mordecai, was most likely born in the captivity; and the events of the book occurred as we have supposed, after the return. Of the education of Mordecai no account is given; but the excellence of his training is sufficiently shown by his conduct and his character. Mordecai was a man prepared, in the ordering of God's providence, for an important exigency in the history of the church; and he was fully able to meet the duties of the case. It is a striking thing in human history that Providence never wants a fitting instrument to further the Divine designs. To the eye of a superficial philosophy, it is the occasion that makes the man; calling forth his energies and enabling him to rise by insensible steps to the summit of complete success. And no doubt there could not be a man without the occasion either forming him to meet it, or formed by him through the energy of his will. But there is a wiser and higher and holier philosophy, that looks beyond the views and the instrumentality of man; and which, discerning the great scope of human history, acknowledges in all, the overruling wisdom of a Divine Providence. This working of God's power in the events of human history may especially be discerned, when we consider these thoughts:

1. The great men of the earth, whether good or evil, alike subserve the purposes of God. Men of different characters, some great in goodness, and some in wickedness; some in ambition, like Alexander, and some in patriotism, like Washington, are raised up for important purposes, and to accomplish great things; and by the instrumentality of both good and evil, God's plans are carried out. The imperfection of our knowledge, and the difficulty of discerning the just relation of one thing to another in

the philosophy of human history, makes the proof of this less full; yet it may be satisfactory. Who can question that Divine Providence raised up such a man as George Washington; and by the exact place and period of his birth; by the precise circumstances of his education; by the wonderful prudence and propriety, rather than by the dazzling brilliancy of his character, fitted him to become the leader of the American armies, and the father of a mighty nation on this Western Hemisphere? And if the mind is disposed to start back from supposing that, by the orderings of that same Providence, the mighty mind of Napoleon Bonaparte was prepared to take a more active, and in one sense, a more splendid part in the troubled revolutions of modern Europe; we need but rise to a higher elevation, and take a wider and larger view of human affairs. We can then vindicate the ways of God to man; we can keep the reins of government still in the hands of the Almighty; and we can see his guidance and control even in the outbreaks of human passions; and in causing guilty revolutions and disastrous wars to effect his purposes. Let it but be remembered, that the God of nations is a God of justice; that war is his scourge, and that the mighty conquerors of earth are as the staff of his indignation to smite the guilty. Isa. x. 5. Was there no cause that the vials of his wrath should be poured out upon France? Was there no reason vindicating the Divine allowance, that a reign of terror should desolate the gay palaces of Paris; that anarchy and discord should cover the vine-clad hills of France; that her sons should melt upon the sands of Sahara, and strew thickly the battlefields of central Europe, and freeze beneath the snows of Russia? There was a long settlement of guilt to make by the God of justice with that people. France became drunk with the enchantments of Rome, that she might persecute the Albigenses; and in the delirium of fanaticism, she poured out like water the blood of her own best children in massacres like that of St. Bartholomew; and this delirium was followed by the insanity of Atheism and the avenging madness of the reign of terror. If there ever was a people to whom it was fitting that Providence should give blood to drink, (for they were worthy of it,) that people was the French; and the terrible wars of which Napoleon was the master spirit; the immense destruction of their people which they willingly endured in the fanaticism of their attachment to him; and their still enduring curse of agitation and restlessness, are the judgments of His hand, who rules the earth in righteousness; and who can use good and bad men to carry out his purposes. The power that raises a man fit for great occasions, just as he is needed, is the all-seeing, all-controlling providence of the mighty God.

2. The workings of his hand in the affairs of human history are further evident from the remarkable fact that the great men of the world can never

themselves project, much less foresee the changes which they are instrumental in effecting.

There is a sense, so far as human agency is concerned, in which human history is one long chapter of *accidents:* great events appear to occur fortuitously, and they surprise the chief actors themselves. But the design is too wise to be ascribed to accident, and even stupid worldlings often admire and say, What hath GOD wrought! Take almost any example in the history of man. When Luther began to preach against indulgences, it was the farthest from his thoughts to break away from the Papal church and to preach the Reformation. He was in heart and soul loyal to the Pope, and idolized the figment of a church with the same fallacy that now deludes a bigoted Romanist, and allows him to put the perverted institutions of Jesus Christ above Christ himself. Luther was led on step by step to the accomplishment of his great work; and the finger of God is seen in the very fact that he knew not for what he was working. The enemies of Luther have cast it up as a reproach, that he professed for a while to acknowledge the Pope, and then threw off the mask. They call him, therefore, a hypocrite. No judgment is more erroneous, or more unphilosophical. Luther acted as men always act who come forth gradually from error to truth; who lose one and another false perception as they advance, and who thus are inconsistent at different periods of life, without being hypocritical. Saul of Tarsus was no hypocrite, though once he destroyed the faith he afterwards established. Luther acted and wrote and effected, just as we might expect in one who had no large plan of his own to accomplish such things; but who was a mere underworkman, often misunderstanding, and never comprehending the designs of the principal Architect. No man, that has the entire matter in his own hands, ever attempts to build a house without settling upon his plan beforehand, and arranging his materials accordingly. Such arrangement Luther did not make. In truth the plan was not his, and the very fact that he went forward not knowing whither he went, and yet succeeded in effecting a Reformation, so much needed and so salutary, is proof that a higher wisdom guided him forward.

But these things are no more true of the great Reformation, than they are of other great changes in the history of man. When the American Colonists took up arms against Great Britain, it was with no design of asserting their independence. The warmest expressions of loyalty were made by some of the most undoubted friends of liberty; the war was in progress for more than a year before the Declaration of Independence was published; and not by the wisdom and foresight of man, but by the gradual leadings of Divine Providence was our path opened to national existence. The thought may be applied not only to great events. It is applicable in a measure to the life and doings of every living man. No man ever yet spent his life according to his own plans for spending it. "A man's heart deviseth his way, but the Lord directeth his steps." God's hand may be traced in the plans of our lives, and in the influences we exert around us; for we are but instruments to carry forward his designs.

The truth then that the results of our most intelligent agency are so largely unforeseen, that step by step each man goes on to unexpected duties and unexpected results, and that usually even the largest usefulness grows not so much from the settled design and purpose to do this very thing, shows the providence of God in preparing men for important places in life. We detract nothing from the honour due to a good and great man who nobly does the duty set before him, nor are we negligent to urge that men should form and prosecute the most earnest plans for doing good. But let us carefully watch providential indications; be ready to embrace them and improve them; and feel that we shall stand most approved before the eye of God, when we have been most ready to do the work he has prepared for us. These thoughts will reappear as we proceed in the narrative.

We may add, 3d, that the workings of Divine Providence in the affairs of men are more clearly seen, if we notice that in every great matter for human good, there are so many different agents, acting at so many different times, and under such different influences, yet all concurring to the one great end, so that philosophically we are forced to acknowledge the presiding mind of one Supreme Intelligence. Look again at the providence of God in the establishing of our own great Republic. Let us suppose that it was the Divine design to establish on this continent the home of true religion and of civil liberty, and to set up a power whose influence should be at once wide and salutary upon the interests of the race. This we firmly and devoutly believe. But the steps to secure this great end imply the omission of so many things which man would have done; the postponement of so many events which man would have hastened; the averting of so many threatening evils which man would have feared; the nice adjustment to each other of so many distinct things and widely separated, which man would have thought not at all connected; and the concentration of so many energies, of times and persons and occurrences, into one point; that Divine wisdom is alone competent to form the plan, and Divine power alone able to carry it into execution. We can name but a few of those strange things which man did not do in the wrong time to defeat God's purposes, and which man did do in the right time to carry out the high designs that man could not possibly foresee. Man did not discover this Western Continent in those ages, before the providence of God had made the needful preparations for planting such a nation as this. Look back over the pathway of history, and put your finger on the time, if you can, so fit for the discovery of America by Columbus as the very period when it occurred. Had this discovery been made one hundred or one thousand years before, the superstitions of Popery and the gloom of the dark ages would have covered two continents instead of one; the mighty energies of Europe, which were misspent to carry on the Crusades, would have borne their hordes of men across the broad Atlantic, rather than the length of the Mediterranean; and would have employed their fanaticism more disastrously for human interests than against the Saracen, in converting the pagan Indians after the mode that Spain converted Mexico, and in subduing these fair territories to the authority of the triple crown; and in such a case the increased power of the man of sin would have held the yoke of bondage for longer generations upon the necks of men.

Again, the declaration of American independence did not occur one year too soon or too late. Had our forefathers declared themselves free and independent, and maintained their stand at a period earlier by twenty-five years, it would have been a calamity deeply to be regretted. If in 1757 the entire territory on North America claimed by the sovereigns of Europe, had been divided into twenty-five parts, the French claimed and seemed to possess twenty parts, the Spaniards four, and the English one.* If instead of the old French war, the en-

* Bancroft's U. S., iv. 267.

ergies of the colonists had been employed in waging hostilities with the mother country for their freedom, and the conflict had been successful, the territory secured to the new government and to the rule of Protestant principles wonld have been no larger, at the most than the old thirteen States. During that old French war, Canada and our entire north western territory and even western Pennsylvania were wrested from the French. What a different destiny had belonged to the North American Republic if all the lands north of the St. Lawrence and of the Ohio, had remained in the hands of the Romanists! What prospect had there been of a great Christian state, rising here to power, and wealth, and freedom, and influence, if, with Quebec and Montreal, with Fort du Quesne, and Detroit, and St. Louis, with Natchez, New Orleans, Mobile, Pensacola, and St. Augustine, three sides of our narrow confines had been surrounded by a cordon of garrisons, officered by the Jesuits? And the successful declaration of American independence twenty-five years earlier would have secured this result. Little did England suppose in that old war that she was fighting a battle for a nation like this, which at no subsequent time could we have fought for ourselves; for it is by the possession of these territories that we have acquired the strength to retain and enlarge them. Just as little did the men who took these preparatory steps, foresee the great end towards which they all tended, as the prattling child, with tottering steps, foresees the active and earnest engagements which his manhood brings upon him. And shall we regard these matters as occurring by chance, because evidently no man had the planning of them? No, we cannot! The God of Providence laid his designs, noted the proper time for each occurrence, raised up proper instruments as each was needed, blessed this people with wise rulers, overruled even the wickedness of men, and we trust, will be *our God for ever and ever.*

But we return from these reflections to speak of the man, whose history called them forth. We suppose that Mordecai, during the four years that passed from the divorce of Vashti, until the marriage of Esther, had secured some humble employment connected with the palace; for he sat in the King's gate. This was doubtless to enable him the more easily to learn the estate of Esther, or perhaps by her favour, that a quiet communication might be carried on between them. His position here gave him an opportunity to detect a conspiracy against the king's life. Life in a palace has its dangers as well as its luxuries, its cares as well as its dignities. What provocation had been given to the conspirators, or injury inflicted upon them, we are not informed. Perhaps they were the mere tools of some noble aspirant to the throne. Judging by the king's hasty wrath against Vashti, it is not unlikely he had given occasion to their anger. We are not to expect true peace or solid friendship in such spheres of life. Where persons form for each other a true and lasting attachment, they must be more upon an equality; at least there must be less room for dependence and fear, than exists between a courtier and a despot. Without denying that true loyalty and even affection may exist for such a monarch, we must own that he stands in great personal danger, from the passions or the fears of his very attending servants.

Mordecai discovered the plot against the life of the king. As a captive Jew, he might have felt not bound in honour or conscience to reveal it; he might even have looked upon the king as the oppressor of his own people, and have joined in the plot for his destruction. But it is one thing for a captive to assassinate a ruler, and quite another to rise up in arms with his captive brethren to vindicate their freedom. And this prince had been no more rigorous against the Jews than others had been, or his successor might be. Besides, the prophets of God had expressly commanded the Jews to seek the good of the country where they were. And now that his beloved Esther was the wife of the king, Mordecai was more earnestly loyal.

Mordecai discovered the plot, and having communication with Esther, he made it known to the ears of the king, through her means. It was one of the follies of the Persian monarch, that few persons had direct access to him; and any attempt on the part of Mordecai to give warning through others at court, might have ended only in failure to reach the king at all, and in the destruction of the informer. In signifying the tidings to the king in Mordecai's name, Esther appears anxious to secure some advantage to him; but it seems strange that she does not take the most natural way for it. Why did she not tell her royal consort, that, when she was an orphan child, this Mordecai had been to her as a father; and ask his aid to repay her debt of gratitude? When this signal benefit had been done to her and to her husband, by defeating the plot against his life, why did she not say, The man who discovered this is my kinsman? The explanation tells us the modesty and humility, perhaps the faith of Mordecai. He forbade it. It tells us as much of the respect and love he had won from Esther, that the queen was still obedient to his wishes, as she had been when under his roof and in his power.

The detected conspirators were punished; but it was a trial of faith to Esther and Mordecai that no special notice was taken of him by whose information they were defeated. Record was made of the fact; a poor recompense for so eminent a service. For who would read those musty pages, or care for the barren acknowledgment to an obscure individual? And to us there seems no connection between this record and the train of the narrative. Yet we shall afterwards see, that this very deed of Mordecai and the modesty which forbade Esther to press his claims for preferment, are made the nice and important hinge upon which rests and turns the issue of a great victory. And here indeed is an invaluable lesson of human life. There are no trifles in character and conduct. There is scarcely an evil deed or word or thought in all our past history whose importance or whose connections for mischief, we are able to trace; and any one, for all we can do to hinder it, may start forward, at some unexpected moment, into remembrance and prominence to punish our sinfulness. There is scarcely a good deed or thought or word in the past, though we may have esteemed it forgotten, useless, or unrequited, that may not start forward, like a seed buried in the dust of a long drought, but now quickened into life and energy and usefulness, greater than our most ardent hopes. Our deeds and thoughts are the seeds of things; as to quantity no man can possibly tell how much fruit a seed will yield; as to its nature, every seed brings forth its own kind. Wicked thoughts or wicked deeds never blessed any man in themselves, or in their fruits. Happy was it for Mordecai, when the chronicles of the empire were read before the king, that the record of his name was blended with a good and not with an evil deed, and that his reward was accordingly. And happy for us, when the records are examined of a greater empire, when the books shall be opened before the sleepless King of kings, if our names, which are surely recorded there, if our deeds, which in that day shall surely not be forgotten, shall call forth the smile of approval from our Eternal Sovereign, and the blessed mandate to the waiting angels, "Clothe with the royal apparel of everlasting righteousness, and deck with a crown of unfading glory, the man whom the king delighteth to honour." There are chronicles whose records never fade! May our names and deeds, however humble, be so written there as to appear unto glory and honour and immortality and eternal life.

But we pause here again for a concluding reflection.

What reason now had Esther to thank and praise the God of her fathers! But a little while ago, a captive and an orphan; and holding that dangerous possession for a friendless girl, the pearl of beauty! and now she sits upon the throne, the queen of Persia! How dazzling the elevation! how splendid her success! Ah brethren! that is a dangerous mistake indeed; yet it is one often made by man in his estimate of human life. Why do we even allow ourselves for one moment to think, that the most elevated positions in life can add dignity to its possessor? The true dignity in every case belongs to the man, to his qualifications, to his virtues, to his becoming behaviour in his place of influence. Place and power are not themselves the objects of envy; a man elevated to a post he is unable to fill, is degraded in the eyes of all beholders. Every advance in life has its risk; the higher a man is lifted, the more we expect of him; and a statue of giant size when near the ground, dwindles to a pigmy upon a lofty pillar. No greater calamity can befall any man than to be called from an humble sphere of usefulness he is competent to fill, to a place of dignity which he has not the capacity to adorn, and where his defects are lifted into public notoriety. Well says the poet,

> "Honour and shame from no condition rise;
> Act well your part: there all the honour lies."

But elevated condition increases responsibility and demands more earnest efforts. It remains to be seen concerning Esther, whether her elevation to a throne is to be a blessing or a curse to herself and others. If virtue remains the brightest diamond in her coronet; if the pearls of modesty, humility, and piety still compose her necklace; if her adorning is a meek and quiet spirit; and if a useful train of good deeds accomplished, follows the footsteps of the stately queen, then all hail to the Jewish maiden's coronation!

And just so with us. The value of life and of any position, any wealth, any honours, we hold in it, will depend upon the use we make of them. Your responsibility to God lies in this very thing—that you are using well the advantages given, not to your neighbour, but to you. Your soul! are you securing its salvation? Your time! are you using it to prepare for eternity? Your influence! is it exercised for good in a world where it is needed? "He that is unjust in the least is unjust also in much." If you are not living and feeling and doing right, just in that position where God has placed you, you would be equally, and possibly more, delinquent in any desirable circumstances for which you long.

LECTURE III.

HAMAN, THE MAGNIFICENT.

THE scene changes; and a new character, destined to act an important part in this eventful history is introduced to our notice. He comes forward with high claims upon our reverence; and demands from us the bow of respect. The foundation of his claim is the fact that he is the favourite of the king; but too often the favourite of a monarch is a selfish minion, deserving only the hatred and the contempt of the people. It is almost a necessary evil in the courts of despotic princes, that there is no access to the ear of the king for the voice of wholesome truth; that the chief aim of his courtiers is to flatter his vanity and thus secure his favour; and that better men are crowded away, because to such fawning and falsehood they will not stoop. It is proof sufficient that a despotism is an unnatural, as well as an unwholesome state of society, when it thus tends to elevate bad men rather than good; and when the proverb is so often verified, that "truth is seldom found in the palace of kings." We have already seen and shall again see the proof that this king Ahasuerus was neither a great, a wise, nor a good man; and though he was blessed in Esther with a wise and pious wife, through whose influence he was sometimes led to the right, we have proof here of his folly and weakness in these facts, that he had a man at court who was his favourite; that this favourite was chiefly eminent for his vanity and his vices; and that especially to such a weak, bad man, without inquiry and without restraint, the king should commit the control of schemes so vast and important.

But let us not anticipate. Our first attention may be turned to the man himself, and to his race and connections, as furnishing a key to subsequent transactions. This man's name was Haman. Eastern names are significant more frequently than among us; and if traced to a Persian root, this name signifies the *splendid*, or the *magnificent*. HAMAN THE MAGNIFICENT is a title to which such a man would eagerly aspire. As to origin, he was an *Agagite*. We know not where to ascribe this name, except to the ancient race of the kings of Amalek. It is no disproof of this, that in the apocryphal chapters of this book, Haman is called a Macedonian; it rather proves that these chapters are of more recent date, when the kingdom of Macedon had become powerful by the ability and success of Philip and Alexander. The opinion that, as an Agagite, Haman was a descendant of Amalek, is as old at least as the days of the Jewish historian

Josephus, who expressly affirms it. Who the Amalekites were, we can easily learn. They were among the most ancient people upon the face of the earth; they are mentioned by Moses as early as the days of Abraham, Gen. xiv. 7; and they are called by Balaam *the first of the nations*. Num. xxiv. 20. Between them and the children of Israel the enmity was long continued and mortal. They were the first people with whom the Israelites had a battle after they came forth from the Egyptian captivity; * and their attack upon Moses was so unprovoked and cruel, that Jehovah swore that his people should have war with Amalek from generation to generation, until, as a people, they should be blotted out from under heaven. It was against this cruel people that the first king of Israel was sent to wage an exterminating warfare; and it was for his sin in sparing them that Saul was rejected from his place. 1 Sam. xv. And after their monarch had been made a captive, it was in righteous retribution for his cruelties, and to fulfil the long-standing curse of Jehovah, that the prophet Samuel "hewed Agag in pieces before the Lord." Though Saul failed to execute his commission, David did much to destroy this people, and perhaps completely broke their power as a nation, when he defeated them after the destruction of Ziklag. 1 Sam. xxx. Yet even then four hundred men

* Exod. xvii. 8. Some suppose this is Balaam's meaning, Num. xxiv. 20.

escaped; and the scattered sons of Amalek, might long afterwards be found among the nations. As Agag was doubtless a common designation of their kings, like Pharaoh among the Egyptian monarchs, and Cæsar among the Roman emperors, Haman was probably a descendant of the royal line; though the words of Samuel may perhaps forbid us to regard him as the descendant of the king whom that prophet slew. The pride of birth for so ancient a people, and such a long line of royal descent, may have been maintained for many generations after Amalek was scattered; especially when the weakness of the fallen family gave no cause of jealousy in the lands where they were exiled. Indeed Haman possesses before us just such a character as we might expect, in one who plumed himself upon his ancient pedigree, and had little else to recommend him.

But this man, Haman, of polite manners and flattering lips, is the favourite of the Persian court; king Ahasuerus advances him above all other princes; and the king's servants bow down to reverence him. This usually follows as a thing of course; nor is it always wrong. There is a respect due to men in high places; and it is proper to reverence according to their office those that are in authority. But how empty and shallow is the applause often bestowed upon such favourites! The smiles that met the eye of Haman were no index of the inner homage of the heart; but the flattery of sycophants, who had learned in the court

> "To crook the pliant hinges of the knee
> Where thrift may follow fawning."

But as in chemical experiments, a few drops in the retort will sometimes change entirely the colour, and even the qualities of the liquid it contains; so, envious flatteries turn to bitter hatred at the first breath of adversity; and the men who now bow so obsequiously before Haman's robes of purple, will soon be as ready to point the way to Haman's ignominious gallows.

But there was one man in the court of Persia who saw the splendour of HAMAN THE MAGNIFICENT, and yet "bowed not nor did him reverence." Though urged to do it by motives of self-interest and personal safety, by the command of the king, and by daily solicitations from both friendly and hostile voices; this man, who standing alone was beneath the scorn of Haman, who held only an inferior post in the gate of the palace, uncovered not his brow and bowed not down his head at the approach of the favourite. Yet there is something here far different from stubbornness or incivility. We miss it much, if we admire only the independence of Mordecai in his behaviour before Haman. It may be true that this man Haman was unworthy of the respect he now demanded; that only by the partiality of a deluded king was so proud and cruel a man in such a station; and that Mordecai was right in refusing to act the hypocrite before a man whom he clearly understood and thoroughly despised. But his resolute independence is dictated by a deeper and more worthy feeling. Mordecai acted thus for conscience sake. He saw in Haman a hated Amalekite; a man abiding, with his race, under the just curse of Israel's God; and before such a man he had no respect to show, no homage to pay. It is true Haman was now possessed of great power; and Mordecai might easily know that he would be disposed to use it, not simply for his personal destruction, but for the peril of all the Jews. Herein is the very strength of Mordecai's faith: that he will not violate his conscience, nor give any tokens of a respect he does not feel, though he knew that the Agagite would soon notice his disrespect; would learn his Jewish kindred; and would, in all likelihood, kindle his rage against the Jewish people. But Mordecai's faith rests upon the covenant of his God. The power now is in the hands of an enemy to his race; but he fears not that power so long as he knew Jehovah's recorded curse against the Amalekites, and Jehovah's recorded covenant for his chosen people. We admire the courage and resolution of Mordecai when we trace it to such an origin. It is a principle indeed rather of the Jewish than of the Christian economy; in our age we know no race so under a special curse that we must avoid all intercourse with them. But it is in him the settled principle of a conscientious man, who knows no reason for consulting his safety or his popularity by bowing before an enemy of God; who even for the protection of his entire people chooses rather to trust in the Lord than to put confidence in such a prince. And we may not omit to add that Mordecai was not mistaken in the estimate he put upon Haman. The Agagite wanted but an opportunity to show that he had all the antipathies of his people against the living God; and that he was fully disposed to do all in his power to crush the chosen people.

The conduct of Mordecai could not long remain unnoticed by Haman. The man could doubtless have remained concealed in the crowd of unregarded attendants on the court; and perhaps with all the evil instincts of his race, the striking features of the Jew might not have attracted the Amalekite's attention, if he had not brought observation upon himself by his singularity. A single spot of ink upon a sheet of white paper; a single fertile spot in a desert; a single light in a wide waste of darkness; or a single star in a cloudy sky, will attract immediate attention; and Mordecai is singled out, because he is unlike the bowing crowds around him. It seems the extreme of rashness in such a man, thus to draw towards himself the fixed gaze of such a prince, whose absorbing feelings, derived by long inheritance from his royal line, are pride of station and vengeance against the Jews. Is not this man rash to provoke the hatred of ages, and to sting the pride of a mortal and powerful foe? Yes, both rash and foolish; if we introduce not another reflection: that *conscience* dictated the resolute action of Mordecai, and *faith* sustained him in it. And shall not this man escape from the very insignificance of his position, compared with the exalted dignity of Haman? Are not scorn and contempt, vices sufficiently kindred to pride, to allow that a worm may insult Haman and yet not be crushed beneath his haughty heel? However this may be, the other element, to which we have alluded, comes in here to embitter this conflict; to enlarge its boundaries; to make it no longer a personal, but a national affair; to elevate it into a conflict in which were involved the religious interests of all succeeding time; to introduce the faithfulness of Jehovah himself as a party in the strife; and far beyond the stretch of Haman's thoughts, to secure his certain downfall. It was no insignificant word that was addressed to Haman's ear when it was told him that Mordecai was a JEW. Ages of implacable hatred were embodied in the word; the revenge of his smitten ancestry and his scattered people seemed placed within his reach; and this important line expresses the deep feeling of Haman, "He thought scorn to lay hands on Mordecai alone."

His resolution is taken to destroy the entire nation of the Jews. But the vain superstitions of paganism, invoked to his assistance, are overruled in the orderings of Providence, for salutary purposes. The heathen, in ancient and modern times, have been accustomed to regard what they call lucky and unlucky days; and to look for the success or failure of their enterprises, according to their auspicious or unhappy beginning. Among the Chinese, now, the burial of a friend will sometimes be postponed for days and even for many months, if the priests cannot determine a lucky day and a lucky place for the interment. We do not even need to go so far as China. Among a people of better religious light and higher civilization than the Chinese, there is one day of the week which prevalent superstition has marked as unfortunate above all the rest; and paganism has hold enough upon the heart of many a Christian, to prevent him from beginning any enterprise upon a Friday. Haman had this superstition; and the lot was cast before him "from day to day and from month to month to the twelfth month," to find a lucky day for his undertaking. We understand that, as in the case of Achan, first the tribe of the unknown transgressor, and then the family, and then the man, were determined by lot, Josh. vii.; so here first the names of the months were put in the urn, and then the numbers of the days, and from these the selection was made. The day pointed out for Haman was lucky indeed; but not for him; nor in the sense he meant it. Haman is fighting against the God of heaven; and "there is no wisdom nor counsel against the Lord." In the orderings of that Providence where no event occurs by chance, the last month of the year and the thirteenth day were chosen; nearly a year must elapse before the dawning of that great day. Thus full opportunity was given to Mordecai and Esther to lay their plans in opposition to his; and to the Jews to prepare for flight or defence. God causes "the wrath of man to praise" him. An earlier day might have been disastrous. The very deliberation of Haman's malice gives occasion to his failure, and signalizes the prophet's words, "The Lord is known by the judgment which he executeth; the wicked is snared in the work of his own hands." Psa. ix. 16.

The agency of the king is needed for the next act in these eventful scenes. How well Haman had calculated upon his credulous confidence, may be seen from his fixing upon the day for the indiscriminate massacre of all the Jews in the empire, before he had secured the royal consent. We may well mourn for the lamentable lot of any people over whom reigns such a heartless monarch as Ahasuerus. Elsewhere indeed he gives evidence of excellent qualities; and in the end he becomes the protector of the Jews; but no acts of rectitude or of compensatory justice can atone for the inexcusable thoughtlessness—to use the lightest term—of a decree like this. A mighty king, the ruler over a hundred states, with the lives of millions at his disposal, without inquiry and without reserve, delivers thousands of his subjects to death with an unconcern that scarcely a wealthy shepherd would show in ordering the brute members of his flock to the slaughter. We make no apology; we know of none that can be made for the king of Persia. The only semblance of it, is his full confidence in his prime minister; and doubtless the Agagite made an artful representation to gain his point. But the proposal to massacre an entire people should have excited the king's attention under any disguise; and if, when excited by wine and surrounded by revelry, the queen may not be divorced without a conference with his counsellors, it is strange that a matter of this magnitude should cost not a single thought, and be thus summarily committed to the caprice of a favourite.

Haman presented his request with subtilty; expecting doubtless that it would be harder to secure than he really found it. His representation respecting the Jews contained just sufficient truth to make it plausible, to carry conviction to an indolent and inattentive mind; and yet it was a false and malicious statement of the true standing of that people. He spoke of a race of men scattered abroad among all the provinces; having laws of their own, different from the usual laws of the empire; disposed to set the laws of the king at defiance; and able from their scattered condition to stir up rebellion against the king's authority. It is refutation sufficient of all these charges to say that afterwards it was by no serious denial of them, that the Jewish deliverance was effected. If the mind of Ahasuerus, as a wise and politic king, had at this time been intelligently convinced by the arguments of Haman, then the judgment would not have been reversed, nor the Agagite condemned to death upon the mere discovery that his beloved queen was one of the destined victims. If the original judgment was just, it was an accident on the part of Haman to include Esther; and the result is proof enough, that the king made no inquiry into the matter, and rested his decision upon no pondering of weighty arguments.

We may be free to acknowledge, that in the plea of Haman against the Jews there was a partial exhibition of truth; yet so used as to do that people the grossest injustice. Unquestionably they had laws diverse from the laws of the realm; and maxims superior in excellence to all that Persia knew; and ideas of freedom greatly differing from the usual ideas of arbitrary kings; and conscientious convictions such as no exercise of tyrannical power could overcome. But all these were qualities of sterling excellence, which every wise prince should know how to appreciate; which might make them formidable to tyrants, but only the more valuable as the subjects of an upright prince. That ruler over any people who is jealous of upright and sterling virtues, that may even sometimes come in conflict with his own plans, is fit to govern only beasts, and not men. A ruler of men should wish them to be men, and should aspire to govern them as such. For, the true policy is, that the higher the dignity of the state in the character of its citizens, the higher rank does the ruler take among the princes of the earth. The king of a million savages is a less dignified potentate than the ruler of a thousand enlightened freemen. For the character and not the number of a people gives dignity to the commonwealth. These indeed may be ideas far above the thoughts of the Persian king; but they are just, and the justice of them should have given the amplest protection to the exiled Jews.

We may notice that all these events occur in that natural order which belongs to current events around us; and that the wickedness of Haman, like the daily wickedness of our times, expects to find success in the use of appropriate measures. Ahasuerus was easily persuaded; but Haman was prepared to give plausible reasons for the measures he proposed. Every scheme of wickedness has its apologies; so much so that men ought to suspect every scheme too fairly presented, and stand in doubt of the man who is the smoothest in his apologies.

Haman's personal influence secured the consent of the monarch; and the large amount pledged to the treasury is surrendered as of no importance. Had Ahasuerus been a wise and prudent prince, the offer of so large a sum of money would have awakened suspicion, and called forth inquiry. The truth is, Haman overshot the mark. Men never bid so high without some great object to gain. And as wicked men often contradict themselves, there was an inconsistency in the statements of the crafty Agagite. He represents the people as unprofitable to the king; and yet offers to pay for their destruction, an immense amount of money as compensatory of the loss the empire would sustain. Surely Haman had here overreached himself, had he addressed any, but the partial ear of a foolish monarch. But favouritism is blind and deaf; and if the king saw at all, it was with a morbid vision, which magnified the generosity of Haman, and refused to take advantage of it. The king can afford to be as liberal as his servant; and Haman receives the credit without the cost of his offer. Even this, however, with every other early success, aggravates the coming downfall.

We are so accustomed to a man's own proper signature to every document, that it requires a moment's reflection to recall, that, if the art of printing is of modern invention, the arts of reading and writing are so connected with it, that they never were in very general use before the era of the printing press. The reported ignorance of days far later than the times of Ahasuerus, may excite our supreme amazement. Noble princes and dignified ecclesiastics too ignorant to write their own names were common personages in Europe but a few centuries ago; the very word *signature* is derived from the fact that the majority, from inability to do more, made a sign or mark; and the seals we affix were once the most certain pledges of a genuine subscription. We cannot argue that the king of Persia could not write; but he had adopted the usual practice of subscribing public documents by a seal or ring. Some of these ancient seals may now be found in any important museum; and engravings of them are frequent in modern commentaries. (See page 80.) In Persia yet, documents are authenticated by the seal, rather than by a signature. The king gave his seal to Haman. He had thus the power to give authority to any proclamation; and this in a realm where even Ahasuerus could not repeal the most absurd and mischievous decree. Thus far the success of Haman seems complete. He has full authority to issue the irreversible command.

The decree was prepared and sent forth to the governors in the wide empire of Persia, written in the king's name and sealed with his seal. The letters were sent by post. The word comes from the Latin *positus*, placed; because by placing horses at certain stations, messages were carried without delay and at great speed to any required distance. There is an interesting section in Rollin's Ancient History where the establishment of the first posts and couriers is ascribed to Cyrus, king of Persia. That prince appointed postmasters to receive the packets, and provide horses; and the riders went night and day without regard to weather. Herodotus speaks of these posts with admiration in the times of Xerxes. But we incline to believe that to the

Jews is due the credit of this invention. It is very certain that no ancient nation exceeded the Jews in general intelligence among the people. We have no good reason to say that permanent arrangements existed among the Jews for transmitting regular intelligence; but posts are mentioned in the Jewish Chronicles in the days of king Hezekiah, a century and a half before the reign of Cyrus; 2 Chron. xxx. 6; and it would be no wonder if Daniel, a Jew and the chief minister of Cyrus, transferred a Jewish institution to Persian practice, to the great admiration of Greek historians, and to the great advantage of the entire world; for this method of communication has now expanded into one of the most important agencies of modern civilization, THE POST OFFICE, than which nothing has done more to fulfil Daniel's own prophetic words for these ages, "Many shall run to and fro, and knowledge shall be increased." Dan. xii. 4. We are so accustomed to the privileges of the Post Office, that we seldom reflect on its advantages. Posts in their origin were not used for the public benefit, but were designed to transmit the despatches of the government. So the decree was sent to the governors. Yet as no secrecy was designed, its purport was made public. All the vile passions of men were let loose against the Jews. It was made lawful for any man whom envy or revenge or cupidity might arouse against his Jewish neighbour, to destroy his family, and to seize on his property. Nor need we think that the very cruelty of the decree would defeat it. The pages of human history prove only too fully that the most inhuman tyrants do not lack willing helpers to execute their schemes. It is impossible for us to realize how latent iniquity in human hearts is restrained by law and custom. The tendency of allowed crime, and especially of legalized crime, to increase, even in men whose principles might be thought to be better, is strong proof that firm restraint should never be relaxed. Philosophers tell us that beneath the crust of the earth there are immense magazines of explosive and combustible materials, and vast internal fires; and in a favourable opportunity these might easily effect the conflagration, and even the destruction of the globe. In proof of this, they point to those volcanic fires which occasionally give partial vent to these energies in the awful eruption, or the terrific earthquake. And so the Scriptures tell us, that the heart of man is the seat of evil passions, deceitful and desperately wicked; and in proof we have records of human sin, which make us tremble and blush that we too are men, and have these hearts of deceit. Had the decree of Haman been carried into effect, it would not have lacked executioners, delighting in the license of blood and cruelty.

Yet sympathy, grief, and indignation would not be wanting in the minds of the better part of the people every where. The Jews had been long scattered: they were thoughtful, industrious, and moral among the heathen; and like light in darkness, their high and holy views of God and of man's duty, must have attracted attention in realms of paganism; and they had doubtless formed many ties of friendship and good neighbourhood. Thus summarily condemned to confiscation and death, without trial and without charge, they became the subjects of a wide-spread sympathy. "The city Shushan was perplexed." This was doubtless an example of the whole empire. Perhaps many Jews resided there; and being near the court, the reason for the decree was better conjectured. Yet if they did know Mordecai's insult to Haman, his revenge must have seemed stupendous.

"And the king and Haman sat down to drink." But little sympathy exists here between the prince and the people. The true theory of government makes all one body; the ruler the head and the people the members. Here the body is perplexed, and the head is indifferent to the sorrows of the members. We do not suppose the words denote any special revelry, as if Ahasuerus or Haman needed to drown the thoughts of a wicked transaction in the oblivion of intoxication. It simply expresses their indifference to the agitation produced by their decree. As for Ahasuerus, having given the entire matter into the hands of Haman, he thought little of it; and the time had not yet come for Haman to be troubled. The consciences of guilty men will often sleep during the longest progress of villany; but when the iniquity has either finally failed, or is successfully done, conscience rises up in terror against the peace of the soul. If sinful men could only see their sins as they will one day see them, and as even in this life they sometimes see too late, they would withhold their hands appalled. Haman's time had not yet come. He was hurrying forward to secure his end, unknowing that his own feet should fall into the deep pit he had digged. Shushan was in perplexity; but the authors of their trouble sat down to drink.

ORIENTAL SIGNET RINGS.

LECTURE IV.

THE IRREVERSIBLE DECREE.

CAN we really give credit to the historical statement here made, that so heartless and cruel a decree should go forth from any monarch against his own subjects—an inoffensive and industrious population—as that recorded of king Ahasuerus against the Jewish exiles? Even supposing that this historical narrative is verified by far more than the usual evidences, which lead us to believe the records of the past, may there not be doubt cast over the whole transaction, by the very extravagance of cruelty here attributed to the monarch and his adviser? May we not say, from our knowledge of human nature, that the heart of man is not capable of deeds so arbitrary and tyrannical? Or if we suppose that such deeds have ever happened, how far back in the annals of the world must we go; to what climes and ages of barbarism; under what debasing and sanguinary forms of religion, must we look; and what are the exciting causes which provoke such iniquity? Alas! the doctrines of the Bible and the gloomy teachings of history—in these pages and out of them—are only too much alike, when they give us the darkest views of human nature, and point us to a hidden source of deep depravity in man himself as the only satisfactory solution of earth's scenes of cruelty and blood. Early in the history of Adam's fallen race have we these impressive teachings, " God saw that the wickedness of man was great in the earth, and that every imagination of the thoughts of his heart was only evil continually." Gen. vi. 5. Before this God had said to the serpent, " I will put enmity between thee and the woman, and between thy seed and her seed." Gen. iii. 15. In these two verses, we have the key to all the cruelties and oppressions of man ; and especially to the remarkable fact that the cruelty of man has never been more fierce than when it has raged against the church of God. We may go far back in history, if you please ; and among its first records and in its very first mention of blood-shedding we have a religious feud, and the innocent and the inoffensive falling before the guilty. What a picture is that! The first born of men is the first murderer, the first persecutor for religion's sake: the first man to die is the first martyr of piety ; and we read no sooner of an altar smoking to the God of mercy, than we hear a voice of blood, crying out from the new-stained earth to the God of justice. And the war thus early begun, has never ended: and as it began between brother and brother, as the seed of the serpent and the seed of the woman sprang from the common mother, so no ties between king and subject, between friend and friend, are regarded in this fatal strife. The brother betrays the brother to death; the father, the son; the children, the parents. Are these strange scenes in human history, so that the iniquity of Ahasuerus must be discredited for want of a parallel? Look back less than two thousand years to that Roman emperor whose name has become proverbial for tyranny, who wished that all his subjects had but one neck that a single stroke might end them all; whose character is portrayed by the current charge, true or false, that he set his capital on fire and danced to his own trifling music, in the light afforded; and this man may be found enveloping his Christian subjects in garments dipped in pitch and setting them on fire as miserable torches to illuminate the imperial gardens. We may descend fifteen hundred years later, and landing in the capital of modern, polished, intelligent France, on the morning of August 24th 1572, we may see a king, instructed in the Romish faith, and solemnly called by the authority of the Pope, "His Most Christian Majesty,"—issue and execute a decree for the slaughter of his Protestant subjects, that surpasses in atrocity any that can be found even in the records of kingly crimes. Let indeed the decree of Ahasuerus be justly considered as humane in comparison with this later edict. Even Haman was willing to publish his intentions;

nearly a year's notice was given that the Jews might escape or resist; and he was but carrying on a war that had existed already without a truce for a thousand years. But the decree of the French monarch was against his own best subjects; was in defiance of the most solemn promises and treaties of friendship; was carefully concealed by tokens of kindness up to the very hour when every preparation was made; and burst upon the defenceless heads of the devoted victims like a sudden peal of thunder from a cloudless sky.

The great bell of the palace, used only upon occasions of public rejoicing, gave the signal in the night; the bells of churches, devoted to the God of peace, answered; and the discharge of fire arms increased the tokens of alarm. A white cross, worn on the hat, distinguished the faithful members of the Romish church; their priests, with a drawn sword in one hand and a crucifix in the other, preceded the assassins, and urged them on; and by the dawn of day Paris exhibited an appalling spectacle: headless bodies were thrown from the windows; the streets were filled with carcases; and the gateways were blocked up with the dying and the dead. The miserable king, Charles IX., fired upon the miserable populace from the windows of his palace, disfigured the lifeless body of one of his bravest and most loyal subjects, and uttered his coarse jests over the work his hands had thus done. A potentate of higher religious claims than the king of

France, even the Pope of Rome, ordered public thanksgivings to be made to Almighty God for the massacre of the Huguenots; struck off a medal to commemorate the great event; (see page 103;) and caused a painting to be made, representing the scene, that hangs to this day upon the walls of the Vatican. We might descend within the memory of living men to a period when such teachings of Popery had brought forth their ripe fruit, and see a nation throwing off restraints, and showing that the hearts, not only of despots, but of men as men, are "desperately wicked." The lesson is only too frequently repeated; and we may not reject this record, because it is so unlike man, but the rather strengthen our faith in a narrative that is unhappily so true to nature.

The decree of Ahasuerus went forth; and now the unbending Mordecai passes before us with his clothes rent, with sackcloth and ashes upon him, and uttering a loud and bitter cry. This is no more unusual to express the grief of an Oriental, than petitions or mass-meetings would be among us. No one there thinks of remonstrating with the government; and the loud outcries of aggrieved individuals excite no special surprise. Can we draw back the veil and read the counsels of God? Can we understand why, in the orderings of his Providence, such dark clouds are allowed, even for a little while, to rest upon the righteous; why such sorrows rend their hearts; and why the voice of exultation is heard in the tabernacles of the proud and ungodly? Could not the pathway of the righteous here, be ever a path of light and comfort—of joy and peace; with no triumphs for Haman and for such as he, and no sackcloth and bitterness for the righteous Mordecai? It is in infinite wisdom, even though we may be unable to trace its every line, that Jehovah has arranged the plan of this world's affairs; and has placed us here to know the trials of ignorance and to feel the pangs of adversity. The law of his earthly kingdom bids us walk by faith and not by sight; and we must needs feel our dependence and be exposed to temptation and danger. There is a sense in which the path of the just is a path of light. The pathway of duty is seldom otherwise than clear to those who wish to find it; and faith assures us that this is the path of safety and of final comfort. Faith rests upon a basis holier and more permanent than our present feelings of joy or sorrow; bids us be careful only of our obedience to the Divine will; and gives the assurance that afflictions, meekly endured, shall yield the peaceable fruits of righteousness. Hebrews xii. 11.

Nor do we lack reasonable arguments to show, that God's glory and man's good are greatly promoted by our most severe trials of faith and endurance. Even in the affairs of this life, they are the most useful and valuable men, who have struggled hard for eminence; and have passed through many trials in their checkered experience. During the periods of temptation indeed, we may be deeply dejected, and may fear for the issue; it is in the very nature of trial, that the eye of faith alone can see the end of it; and our faith is not to be estimated by the strong fears and weighty griefs, with which it is brought into conflict; but rather by its efforts to contend against these, and its final triumph over them. During the darkness and terror of a storm at sea, the sailor cannot appeal to the heavens to learn his present position, and the progress he is making; such observations belong to fair weather; but he can still appeal to his compass to tell the direction which he would go. During our seasons of sorrow and trial, God gives us still his word as our compass, and light enough to see the path of duty; he assures us of his continued kindness and protection in spite of adverse appearances; but it is only when the storm is past that we can learn how far it has sent us upon our way; can discern the mercy that sent it; can rejoice that trouble brought us large experience of his kindness, and love, and grace; and can sing the oft repeated song of the royal psalmist,

Yet I have found 'tis good for me,
To bear my Father's rod;
Afflictions make me learn thy law,
And live upon my God.

When these trials are past, and God's ransomed

people are gathered home, his ways of dark providence will be vindicated; we shall see what we should now believe; we shall understand fully what we now comprehend partially; the darkest clouds will have been found by experience to be full of the largest showers of mercy; and things which we thought the worst that could happen, will be found among the best. Let us believe these lessons now. Providence is often to be judged by contraries; when God is kindest, he may seem severe: or rather God is ever to be credited upon the truth of his holy word, which we can read; and not judged by the appearances of his providence, which we cannot read. And it is unquestionably a design in recording such troubles, and the slow-moving but certain period of deliverance from them, to encourage the church and each believer in their trials. For if the actual occurrences of human affairs are different in each age, in each rolling year, and with each individual, so that every man has an experience peculiarly his own; still the principles of the Divine government remain permanent and unchanging. The same covenant-keeping God, who watched over Israel and Mordecai, watches in the affairs of his meanest servant; appoints his angels to minister about their path; and notices the struggles, and rewards the triumphs of their faith. These things are written for our learning; these trials and temptations beneath which we now weep and mourn, are in His full view, who wisely orders their occurrence;

their end is present before him, and a train of means is laid in infinite wisdom to secure its happy accomplishment. Let worldly men be skeptical, if they will, of these kind orderings in the providence of God; rebels against his law, let them fight, like Haman, against his mercy to Israel; blind to their own duty, no marvel, if they are ignorant of his power and grace; but their folly and madness may not rob God's believing people of their delightful privilege. We may still trust his minute and constant guardianship. The book of Esther teaches the same essential lesson which Christ taught his disciples, "the very hairs of your head are all numbered." Matt. x. 30. The lessons of these pages are lessons of confidence in the darkest hours of trial; lessons of rejoicing in tribulation from the prospect, not only of deliverance, but also of enlargement; lessons of peace in hours of grief. Here, long before the days of Paul the apostle, may we learn Paul's great lesson, "We know that all things work together for good, to them that love God, to them that are the called according to his purpose!" Rom. viii. 28.

"Let us be patient! These severe afflictions
  Not from the ground arise;
But oftentimes celestial benedictions
  Assume this dark disguise;
We see but dimly through the mists and vapours;
  Amid these earthly damps,
What seem to us but dim, funereal tapers,
  May be heaven's distant lamps!"

But what judgment are we to form now of Mordecai, when he thus clothes himself in sackcloth, and bewails so bitterly the stern decree? Has his confidence now failed in the covenant promise to God's chosen people? Does he begin to regret his ill-timed boldness, in thus provoking the enemy of his faith and of his race? Is he willing now to bow down, with obsequious reverence, at the feet of the haughty Agagite? Not one of these things is true, as we shall further see in the narrative. And yet Mordecai is in trouble. And to reconcile his lamentations in such a case, with the genuineness and even with the firmness of his faith in God, affords us one of the most important practical lessons of the life of piety; a lesson we are very slow to learn, and yet one we need quite as much as any other, in all the teachings of the Bible; a lesson that comes home to the conflicts and fluctuations of our own breasts, and bids us look forward to the day of triumph. There is no foundation in the word of God for the idea, that faith destroys our humanity, that it steels the heart against all fears, and quells the risings of all timidity. True piety is as far removed from stoical apathy on the one hand, as it is from quailing despondency upon the other. The faith of a pious mind exists in a mind that still remains human; that has yet the misgivings and ignorance, the fears and tremblings incident to man's experience; and when these fears and difficulties abound the most, the strength of faith is seen—not so much in our banishing them from the mind—as in our triumph over them. That is a strong faith, which sees difficulties, weighs them, and fears them; but refuses to be deterred by them from the path of duty.

Mordecai was troubled at the decree. This was not wrong, but perfectly natural. God designs that we should feel our adversities, should mourn at the frowns of his providence, and then roll our care upon him. Nor must we forget an important matter, which entered as an essential element into Mordecai's humiliation. He mourned for the calamities threatening his people. If personal differences only had existed between himself and the Agagite, it may be, Mordecai would have acted otherwise. Or had the haughty foe of his faith singled him out as a Jew, the solitary object of his hatred, he would perhaps have gone even to death with the spirit and bearing of a martyr, scorning the hereditary foe, and rejoicing to die for his faith; and no cry of bitterness would have wailed through the streets of Shushan; no pang of regret would have rent the heart of Mordecai, as he passed to join the noble army of witnesses, who have sealed with their blood the testimony of God. But the nation of Mordecai was involved in the revenge of Haman; and however firm was the faith of this heroic man in the final issue of Israel's triumph, it was impossible for him to foresee at how great a cost to his people this new conflict might be. It was no light thing to

Mordecai, that upon him lay the responsibility of provoking the conflict; and though well assured of the rectitude of his principles and the sincerity of his motives, he could not repress some anxious solicitude for the measures he had taken; some earnest searchings of heart to see whether he might not have fulfilled his entire duty to God without involving Israel in trouble like this. Times of severe trials lead us to search our motives; and even when we judge that we have done as we ought—that if things were again to do, we would pursue the same course; we may yet see reason to mourn the calamities our faithfulness may have brought upon others.

The first tidings of the decree greatly distressed Mordecai. Regardless of appearances, he ran through the streets in wild excitement, bewailing even to the gates of the palace, the calamity of his people. But he does not spend all his strength in vain lamentations. Strong emotions cannot last long; and it is well they cannot. Mordecai is as deeply grieved afterwards, but his mind becomes more composed; he carefully considers how the threatening storm may be averted; and he earnestly sets to work to carry his plan into execution. That grief which unfits us for duty is inordinate and unsubmissive; while true submission is entirely consistent with the use of measures to secure consolation, when our trials are beyond remedy; and to secure relief from evils, which may be averted.

What are we to say of that sentence upon this

truthful page, "None might enter into the king's gate clothed with sackcloth?" The halls of Ahasuerus were set apart for gayety and mirth; the grotesque robe of the buffoon, or the embroidered cloak that covered the painted hypocrite, might freely enter there; but the coarse, rough clothing that betokened distress and sorrow, was debarred entrance to the palace of the king. Was this too an unalterable decree in the wise realm of Persia? Are edicts fraught with distress unutterable, ever to go forth from those marble chambers, and yet the ponderous gates be never thrown open, that sorrow, or the tidings of sorrow, from a stricken nation or a sinful race, may perchance reach the ear of the king? And can we imagine it possible, that in that abode of splendid tyranny, no sighs were ever heaved, no tears ever fell? When the tidings of Vashti's disgrace fell heavily upon the ear of the beautiful queen, did no thoughts befitting the sackcloth cross her heart? Amid the cruel desolation of so many fair damsels, torn from the abodes of parental tenderness to pine in the harem of the Persian king, were there neither visible griefs, nor secret lamentations? Had the mighty king forbidden his porters to open up at the knock of that impartial messenger, whose dark shadow falls alike upon the threshold of the palace and of the cottage? If one Persian king was angry that the waves of the sea would not do his bidding; shall another frown that death will not stay at his command? Had Ahasuerus forgotten the only wise thing that history has recorded of his father; the memorable weeping of Xerxes at the rapid and resistless march of inexorable death?

Yet we need not wonder at the foolish mandate—Sackcloth may not enter the palace of the king. It would indeed have been wiser far, if the voice of sorrow had often been welcomed there; if sackcloth and mourning had been freely invited guests; if the voice of revelry had given place to an appointed messenger ever sounding, in the monarch's ears, the fact of his mortality; if instead of increasing his people's sorrows, he had been ever ready to hear them, to sympathize with them and to relieve them; and if salutary thoughts of death had prepared Ahasuerus himself to die. But we are not surprised at these words of folly in the Persian court, for the spirit that dictated such an order, is still existing where it finds no direct utterance in such words of folly. Is it not true, that in the halls of modern gayety, in the circles of fashion, in the abodes of luxury, and in parties of vain pleasure, these thoughts of sorrow and mortality are yet guests as unwelcome as the sackcloth garment in the Persian palace? Do not men now banish all thoughts of grief and death, and all preparation for that most certain and most important event? How many of us love to think of that solemn hour, and have made an intelligent preparation for it? And why should we not? Do thoughts of sorrow have any tendency to bring sorrow upon us? When we allow our minds to reflect upon death, can such reflections have any tendency to hasten the footsteps of the final messenger, that he may knock the more speedily at our door? Certainly this is not so.

When the commander of a fortress about to be besieged takes his glass, and examines the number and power of the approaching enemy, it is only apparently and not really, that the danger is brought nearer. He is better able by means of his telescope to discern the peril; to understand how great it is; to prepare to meet it, and perhaps to overcome it; but certainly his clear vision neither hastens the hour of danger, nor increases the danger itself. It is purely an advantage. So, thoughtful contemplation, through the glass of God's holy word, of grief and death, may give us better ideas of sorrow, and prepare us to meet it when it comes; but it can have no effect to increase the power of our troubles over us, nor to hurry forward the visits they make to our abodes.

The true reasons for the decree of Ahasuerus, and for the banishment of serious thoughts from human minds, are the aversion of man's heart to good; the power of conscience that dares not think of death; and the love of those frivolous and often guilty pleasures, that are so easily marred by the sounds of sorrow. Before we curl the lip in scorn at this new token of Persian folly, let us examine whether we ourselves are truly wise on this point. We are in a world of sorrow; let us learn to sympathize with it; to bear it ourselves; to draw precious advantages from it. We are in a world where death reigns; and we are certain, he will one day enter our abodes, and strike at our hearts. Let us be mindful of this mortality. Especially let us make Him our friend, who is death's conqueror, and who gives us a triumph over the grave.

Yet men will go on in this way of folly, still virtually writing over the doors of their theatres, and their ball-rooms, and their parlours and their closets, "Let no one enter here clothed in sackcloth." Vain and impotent decree! If they would shut out SIN the cause of sorrow, and the inventor of the garments of mortal grief, it would be something; but they welcome the cause and wish not the effect; they plant the seed, and wish the tree to be fruitless. But it may not be. Ahasuerus may close his palace gates, and doubly guard them with his most careful officers, but sorrow will enter there in despite of the bars, and steal silently by his most vigilant porters; death, with leaden noiseless step, will tread his tesselated pavements, and shoot his fatal arrows through the costly tapestry; and the page and the peer, the minister and the monarch, unconscious of surrounding splendour or meanness, must be clothed in the garments of the grave. Men may put away from them the thoughts of affliction, but they will come. They may fear sorrow itself, but it will come. They may shrink from the approach of death, but it will come.

They may loathe the silent grave, but there they must come. They may dread the resurrection, but it too will come. They may tremble as they think of judgment, but

"That awful day will surely come."

They may be unprepared for the retributions of eternity, but they will come—come all the more terribly, because they are unwelcome: and when they come, they will endure for ever!

"None might enter the king's gate clothed in sackcloth." Ahasuerus was a great monarch; kings bowed down to do him reverence; millions of subjects obeyed his decrees; and many a heart was bowed in sadness through his wide dominions. But how unhappy was that rule, which in a world of grief and sadness seemed so to forbid all sympathy between the ruler and the ruled! Who would wish to be governed by a monarch whose character is revealed by such a word as this? It is our privilege to dwell beneath the beneficent sceptre of One, whose decree is all the reverse of this. We dwell in the land of a mighty monarch. Our sovereign is the King of kings. On his head are many crowns. All power is given to him in heaven and upon earth; and this power he uses freely to bless the sorrowing, and the voice of grief is ever welcome in his ears. When he dwelt among men in the garments of our humanity, his daily walks were among the children of sorrow; disease and suffering found relief in his healing smile; and he wept with those that were in mourning. The palace on earth where our King has established his throne and dispenses his favours, is the sanctuary of the broken hearted; and no more fitting words could be written upon its portals than his own delightful utterance, "Come unto me all ye that labour and are heavy laden and I will give you rest." Matt. xi. 28. Around his throne of grace, now for more than sixty centuries, have bowed the sackcloth garments of a stricken world: here the tears of penitence have been freely poured out; here the sighs of the broken hearted have been freely vented. And welcome now are all the sons and daughters of sorrow. He has ascended up on high; but not to forget that cardinal principle of his kingdom. He has yet a sympathy with us in all we feel; for he once was in all points tempted like as we are. Heb. iv. 15; v. 7. He once poured out his supplications with strong crying and tears. Well may we rejoice in the gracious invitations of such a King. Many of us have poured our sorrows at his feet; and found that he alone can give true relief. We invite our suffering brethren to come also to him. Come sinful soul! Hear his gracious voice. He calls you, rather than rejects you. Are your sins a burden? Do you tremble in view of the coming judgment? Has earth no solace for a troubled spirit? The sanctuary is a refuge from trouble. Our king welcomes the humbled sinner. None ever trusted in him and were confounded.

Let us not repress the further reflection that there is a palace of this glorious King upon whose gates is written, in truth and not in mockery; by the hand of authority and not of impotent presumption, "None may enter here clothed in sackcloth."

Blessed are all they that do enter in through the gates into that city, where "God shall wipe away all tears from their eyes; and there shall be no more death, neither sorrow, nor crying, neither shall there be any more pain." Rev. xxi. 4. But is it not worthy of remark, that those who most earnestly hope and prepare for an abode in that glorious palace of our immortal King, are such as here make themselves most familiar with thoughts of death? It is not true that wise thoughts of our mortality are as wormwood cast into the sweet fountain of our earthly pleasures to make it bitter. It is a tradition among the Jews, that Moses healed Marah, the fountain of bitter waters in the wilderness, by casting into it a bitter tree. Exod. xv. 23—25. The idea finds its fulfilment here. Earthly engagements are themselves unsatisfactory—a bitter fountain, yielding streams of gall and wormwood. Cast into this Marah in our wilderness, those thoughts of salutary affliction, which are as wormwood to the natural mind; and the pure, sweet waters of consolation and of pious peace flow forth. It is wisdom in us to welcome sorrow and the thoughts of it; for certain it is, that there are no happier hearts on earth than those that are often filled with thoughts of sorrow and dying; and have perhaps the very oftenest been brought into fellowship with these things.

The grief of Mordecai was quickly communicated to Esther; and she sent a message to take away his sackcloth; and when he received not this, to know the cause of his distress. In return Mordecai sent to the queen a copy of the proclamation, which had been issued at the instigation of Haman against the Jewish people. And here enters the first ray of light touching the designs of God's providence in introducing a Jewish maiden to royalty in that empire. The movements of Divine wisdom are slow and deliberate; there is no danger that some unforeseen contingency can thwart his plans. Esther had now been queen more than four years; and eight years and a half have elapsed since the divorce of Vashti; and as yet no apparent advantage has occurred, not even to Mordecai, the orphan's friend and protector. But his faith begins now to discern how God designs to use her for the preservation of his people. His grief operates not to prevent the wise consideration of duty; nor his faith to supersede the careful use of means. He sent word to Esther that she should lay the matter before her royal husband; and make supplication for the safety of her race.

We have no record of the immediate effect of these calamitous tidings upon the queen; but we know that she was distressed for the afflictions of Jacob; and though labouring under some disadvantages, best understood by herself, she was ready to use all the means in her power to bring relief. In reply to Mordecai she reminded him that there was a law in the palace, forbidding any person to approach the king unless called so to do. This law shows us the great distance in eastern lands, between the monarch and his subjects. It was perhaps ostensibly enacted to prevent the attacks of assassins whom despotic princes ever need to fear, and to keep up the state of the king; but certainly it seemed to make the king the mere tool of artful officers through whom communications would be kept up with the empire, and who, save as their jealousies would lead them to keep each other in check, would give or withhold intelligence as they pleased. The single exception to the law lay in the will of the king; and he might at his pleasure hold out his golden sceptre, in token of favour, to even an unbidden visitor. But for some reason, unknown to herself, the beautiful queen had not seen the face of her royal consort for an entire month; and perhaps her mind was ready for all manner of conjectures as to the cause. Four years in the palace may have shown her the king's weakness and fickleness; and perhaps have awakened the fear that he would be as ready to divorce her, as Vashti. When she heard of this decree against her people, and put that beside her long exclusion from seeing his face, the fear would certainly not be unnatural that the king designed to exclude her; and that his estrangement had already kept him from her apartments for a month. It is natural in times of distress and perplexity to allow our minds to dwell upon the dark side of every matter; and it was no doubt with many misgivings that Esther pondered the plan which her respected cousin urged upon her.

But his arguments and her resolution will engage our thoughts at another time. We now conclude with a single reflection.

We are called upon earth to a life of faith. We need not expect to pass our time here without sorrow; nor think that God's providence will always smile. Let us not expect to engage in any duties of great importance without being perplexed by difficulties; nor should we even wish that our path should be different from the usual path in which God leads his people. We shall be happiest when we walk in the footsteps of the flock.

Let us make up our minds to acquaint ourselves in the teachings of his word, with what we have to do; and earnestly to do it, in spite of perplexing anxieties and opposing difficulties. Duties are ours; events are God's. The path of devotion and duty is the path of safety. We should not be envious of the peace of ungodly men, or of their apparently superior security. Whatever darkness may surround the dealings of God with our souls, the principles he has given to guide us, are plain enough. His law is our rule of life,—his gospel, the only hope of the guilty.

Let every believer walk humbly before Him and trust the orderings of his wisdom.

Let those who are unreconciled to God, and who rank among his foes, fight no longer in madness against his throne. Let them repent of their evil ways; flee to the foot of Calvary and sue for mercy. We shall see, as we proceed in this history, that the sinner's prosperity but goes before his destruction; and that it is vain to fight against God. Let it be your wisdom, impenitent man, to submit ere it be too late to gain the advantage of it; and find your happiness and your eternal life through that grace, which is freely offered in the name of the dying Son of God!

MEDAL OF THE MASSACRE OF ST. BARTHOLOMEW'S.

LECTURE V.

DIVINE DESIGNS AND HUMAN DUTY.

TROUBLE has entered the marble halls of Ahasuerus, if even sackcloth, its outward symbol, is shut out by law. The decree, which Mordecai sent to the queen, threw her into great perplexity. On the one hand, she was deeply grieved for the calamity that had befallen her unhappy people; and on the other, she seemed suddenly deprived of the power to afford them the slightest relief. The apparent estrangement of her royal husband occurred just at a juncture to fill her with the deepest anxiety. Perhaps his absence from her apartments for thirty days, was the result of design; perhaps it was a proof that her kindred, hitherto concealed, was discovered, and that she was intentionally and by name included in the plot of the wicked Haman. We cannot wonder at Esther's perplexity. It is just such perplexity as we ourselves would feel in such a case; and as nothing more arouses the mind to active energy than circumstances of peril, we would have imagined and feared as she did. In studying the pages of sacred or profane history, we must take an interest in them as the records of human life. Upon no historian can we place so entire reliance as upon these sacred writers; yet must we interpret what they record, with the remembrance that the actors in these scenes were not inspired, though the historians are. The influence of inspiration is, not to lift the actors here above the level of our humanity, but simply to give a truthful representation of what they were, of how they felt, of what they did. And it is just because we have here an exact transcript of human feelings in the trials of human life, that these records are valuable for our instruction; and it is only when we judge of them through the medium of our own feelings, that we form a just estimate of the different characters, and see the wonders of God's providence in governing the free actions of intelligent minds.

But the lessons of wisdom upon these inspired pages are expressed only in principle; and we think it our place to consider these attentively, and more at large than we find them here. Hence we do not hesitate to arrest our progress through the narrative, as occasion offers for profitable thoughts. If the traveller, hurrying forward in his journey, may not stop to pick up every stone that glitters in his path; yet he can well afford to stay long enough to pick up a valuable diamond.

Stopping the course of the narrative for the present, let us consider the argument preferred by

Mordecai, when he would urge Esther to go in and ask the king for the life of her people.

Esther reminded Mordecai of a well known law in Persia, that if any one came in to the king uncalled, his presumption was fatal to himself, unless it pleased the king to hold out his golden sceptre. That such a rod or sceptre of gold was used by the kings of Persia is mentioned by Xenophon. While these profane writers add no authority to the Bible, it is a matter of interest to notice instances where they agree with the statements of inspiration; and there will, we believe, be much corroborative proof of the correctness of the Scriptural writers in the interesting investigations of antiquaries among the ruins of Oriental empires. The first fruits give promise of a large harvest. As Esther had not been called to go in, she naturally feared that her intercession would be fatal to herself. Yet the urgency of the case causes Mordecai to press the matter upon her as an imperative duty.

Now notice here, in the first place, that Mordecai does not attempt to lessen the real difficulties before Esther. He appreciates her position. He saw that she had reason to feel and fear just as she did. He doubtless entertained some of the same anxieties; and his tenderness for her, as well as the dictates of an enlightened judgment, would have avoided all possible difficulties, and have spared her any unnecessary trial. When we set ourselves to perform any duty, it is no mark of wisdom to encounter difficulties, which may as well be avoided; nor yet to undervalue the obstacles which we must surmount. This is true in every case of duty; true no less in the greatest duty to which we are called. Let the man who would follow Christ, in obedience to Christ's own command, set himself down and count the cost. We may not abate any of the difficulties in the way; nor entice men to follow Him by false representations of the ease and enjoyment they may expect. Nothing is more remarkable in the teachings of our Lord Jesus Christ, than his explicit declarations that self-denials must be expected; and his plain forewarnings that in following him, men must take up the cross. No false inducements does he hold out; no compromise of doctrines to be believed, or of duties to be done, does he offer, to win the service of the most influential man. Nothing is really gained by undervaluing the obstacles which lie in the path of duty. Mordecai saw the strength of the arguments urged by Esther; and he neither denied them, nor sought to turn their force aside.

But Mordecai takes too wise a view of the case, and is too deeply interested, to allow these difficulties to deter him from urging Esther further. He recognizes these as difficulties truly; but there are yet greater difficulties and dangers which beset her inactivity in this vital matter. The duty of Esther, like almost all the serious and important duties of life; like, we may especially say, the great duty of the sinner to flee for salvation to the cross of Christ, was a duty, where responsibility and difficulty beset her, whichever way she turned, whether she acted or refused to act. If the soul of an anxious man, troubled and burdened by sin, is afraid to flee to Christ for everlasting life, lest he should be rejected in his earnest suit, such a man in all wisdom should carefully ponder, whether he should not be even more afraid to stand back from an humble application for His grace, in whom alone are hopes of life and salvation. It is some such plea as this that Mordecai urges with the queen of Persia.

Admitting the difficulties which seemed to prevent her efforts to avert the threatened evil, he warns her, in the second place, against entertaining any hopes of her personal safety, if she declines the earnest effort of duty on behalf of her kindred. It is no uncommon thing that the mind of man is swayed at the same time, almost equally, by flattering hopes and desponding fears. Esther had apparently good reasons for flattering herself that she might escape, in the execution of the edict against her people. Her Jewish descent was not known; her abode was in the palace where no hostile foot dared to intrude; she was queen of the realm; she was beloved of her husband. True, she did feel anxious, lest there were some secret workings against even her life; but if there *were* any such, her fate was certain and only so much the earlier, if she ventured to enter unbidden the presence of the king. While Esther pondered the matter, nature would bid her shrink from the serious responsibility thus urged upon her. But the faithful words of Mordecai warn her of the deceitfulness of sin; and remind her that the path of duty and the path of safety ever lie together. "Think not that thou shalt escape in the king's house more than all the Jews." The sleepless enmity of Haman; or the jealous envy of less favoured inmates of the palace; or the frown of that God to whose people she was faithless; or the alarms of an unquiet conscience, would betray the recreant queen, if in this important crisis she consulted her fears, selfishly looked only to her own safety, and flattered herself with hope of exemption in the general destruction of her race.

But we may thirdly notice, that Mordecai urges upon her attention a motive, which faith alone could conceive; and which a pious mind alone would be fully prepared to appreciate. Looking calmly at the promises of God respecting his covenant people, the earnest Jew is firmly persuaded that this dark and threatening storm shall never break for the destruction of Israel. He possesses a calm confidence that the God of Abraham will not allow the enemy to triumph; he has read upon the prophetic scroll the Divine assurance to Zion, "No weapon formed against thee shall prosper;" Isaiah liv. 17; and he has hymned the psalmist's praises, "My covenant will I not break." Ps. lxxxix. 34. Resting his firm faith on the sure foundation of Jehovah's faithfulness, he believes that here is presented to Esther a favourable opportunity to forward the designs of Providence; and that her timely elevation to such a post of honour and influence, had marked her as the person by whom should be effected a glorious deliverance. These important thoughts he presses upon the attention of the queen. Yet what power of faith is here! We can hardly think that this man, whose faith penetrates through the thick darkness now around his people, is the same Mordecai, who lately ran like a madman through the streets of the city, clothed in sackcloth, and bewailing the cruel edict. See the difference between impulse and principle; and learn that if strong feelings sometimes sway the believer, yet his principles will soon assume their wonted control, and a calm and steadfast faith will subdue the wildest storms of grief.

These words of Mordecai are so striking in themselves and they embody lessons so valuable for the instruction of subsequent ages, that we regard it our duty to analyse their wisdom, and to present more plainly the important principles which his argument to Esther involves.

1st, The language of Mordecai expresses his firm conviction that this calamity shall yet be averted from the Jewish people. So he says, "Enlargement and deliverance SHALL ARISE." God had promised the well being of Israel; and it was impossible, to the mind of a believer, that his word should fail. And this is a faith which God's humble servants may yet exercise in reference to the stability and deliverances of Zion in troublous times. "God is in the midst of her; she shall not be moved." Ps. xlvi. 4. His promises are precious, and they are sure; none of them have ever been forgotten, nor is it possible they ever shall be. But his promises regard not only the stability of the church; he pledges as well her enlargement. Look abroad over the destitutions of the heathen world; and while you mourn that the dark places of the earth are full of the habitations of cruelty, while you deplore the apathy of Christians to obey their Lord's ascending command, forget not that certain promise of enlargement and deliverance, "I will give thee the heathen for thine inheritance, and the uttermost parts of the earth for thy possession." Ps. ii. 8. Through all the difficulties that seem to beset Zion; beyond the sleep upon the treacherous lap of the indulgent world that has shorn her of her Nazarite strength; through the dust and clouds and strife of many a stern conflict; let our faith regard the fulfilment of his promises, and exclaim with Mordecai, Enlargement and deliverance shall arise! Happy are they who identify themselves and their interests most intimately with the church of God; for in every conflict the final victory must remain with her. And happy they who cast their souls on the gracious assurances of Zion's King. The voice that calls, "Come unto me all ye that labour and are heavy laden and I will give you rest;" Matt. xi. 28; the voice that says, "Him that cometh unto me I will in no wise cast out," John vii. 37, is a voice we may trust. Every word shall find its fulfilment. It may be through troubles and darkness, through fear and perplexity; but enlargement and deliverance in due time shall come; and they that are faithful in Zion shall share in Zion's glory.

2. The language of Mordecai teaches us, that whatever designs God has formed for the benefit of his people, and whatever promises he has given for our confidence, are to find their fulfilment in the use of proper means, and to be secured through the energy of appropriate agents.

Objections are very commonly made among men against the eternal purposes of God, and against his efficient providence, that the belief of these grand truths leaves nothing for man to do, and interferes even with his voluntary agency. Yet it is well for us to notice that the scriptural writers, who most bring into view the sovereignty of God in purpose and act, recognize no inference flowing from this, to hinder their earnest exhortations to human duty. These objections have never influenced those true servants of God, who may be thought best acquainted with the true influences of these Divine teachings; and indeed they have not the slightest foundation of truth, in a just understanding of God's purposes and dealings with the sons of men. Mordecai firmly expects that

God will protect his people ; but this faith is far from interfering with either his anxieties, or his efforts to secure this great result. He knows this thing will certainly come; but he does not stand by and fold his arms awaiting the movements of Providence, like the rolling forward of the wheel of fate; and even when he contemplates the possibility, that the rescue may come neither by his hand nor by that of Esther, yet he looks not for it as by the shifting of some theatrical scene, the waving of a fairy wand, or the workings of a magical charm. He looks for the desired result through Esther, or from some quarter where man shall work for God. The romantic vagaries of man's wild imagination are far different;—often they are far less wonderful, than the actual working of Divine providence; and the inspired instructions of God's word always teach human duty. The faith of Mordecai embraces the promises of God; but he is not forgetful of the duties which God's law commands, and God's providence indicates. He urges the queen to an earnest effort, that the certain deliverance may come through her means. If indeed Esther holds her peace, Providence will not lack an agent for the Lord's designs. Mordecai here plainly implies, that the providence of God in this world's government is a power that operates efficiently, not without the agency of second causes, nor in defiance of them, but by means of them; and that this truth we must hold in that just balance, which forbids us to neglect God, or to forget his supremacy and efficiency on the one hand; and which on the other hand, equally forbids that we should overlook our own interests and duties, and those connected instrumentalities by which he works. We totally misapprehend the teachings of the Bible, when we suppose that man's duty is lessened by the purposes of God. His purposes and promises do rather establish and encourage our duty; and as we shall further see, in considering these words of Mordecai to Esther, they deter us, by the most serious considerations from all unfaithfulness.

Take even the doctrine of election, as set forth in the Scriptures, and base it, as you should, upon the sovereign purpose of God. The common conception of this doctrine is as much a deformed caricature of the truth, as the supposed influences of it are a perversion of its real influences. Instead of encouraging men in indolence and neglect of duty, this doctrine animates, and commands, and encourages their earnest efforts. God can indeed accomplish his purposes, without man's help and in defiance of man's opposition. But he chooses to work otherwise; and it is a great matter for us to notice that in fact he does set men to work, and does accomplish his ends through that which man may do. This book of Esther is a remarkable exemplification of God's purposes effected without a miracle, and through the agency of men. So he is working around us; so he ever works; so he works in the salvation of souls. God saves the souls of elect men through conversion, and not in neglect or defiance of his own converting grace. For man to use the threadbare cavilling, "If I am to be saved, I will be saved, let me do as I will;" is as great an absurdity as to say, "If I am to be shot, I will be shot, whether the bullet predestined to kill me, hits or misses." Rather, if I am to be shot, it is just as certain, the bullet must hit me. If God designs the salvation of any soul, he equally and thereby designs that that soul shall repent of sin, and renounce it; and shall believe in the Lord Jesus Christ unto salvation. Whenever a man can be killed without dying, or live without life, then may one be saved without conversion; and not till then. When Mordecai, though assured of Israel's deliverance, yet urges Esther to exert herself to secure that result, he teaches a lesson to every sinful man touching the great method of securing his salvation. The means of reaching any end in the purposes of God, are equally purposed with the end itself. Let the sinner forsake his evil ways, and turn to the Lord, for without such a duty discharged on his part, he cannot secure salvation; and let him be encouraged in the duty, because its true discharge is, in the purposes and promises of God, the invariable precedent of eternal life secured. Let the guilty soul flee to Jesus, for there only is salvation; and none ever trusted in him and were confounded. The certainty that God's purposes and promises shall be fulfilled, is the largest encouragement of man's efforts to do God's will, and of man's hope to secure God's blessing. Mordecai looks for deliverance through an appropriate instrumentality.

3d. But there is a third important principle set forth for our instruction in these words of Mordecai, "Who knoweth whether thou art come to the kingdom for such a time as this?" The words seem to refer to the nice adjustment in the providence of God of our opportunities and our agencies. There is generally indeed a greater or less obscurity in our efforts to apply the principles of our duty to the providential changes which are constantly occurring around us. There is therefore a peradventure in the exhortation of Mordecai; and we ever need to feel our dependence upon divine guidance and support. "Who knoweth?" is the position we must ever hold; and thus faith may have its fears. But faith must also have its hopes and its ventures. Mordecai here teaches us, that a providential opportunity for doing or receiving good should be regarded by us as a providential call; and we should humbly and firmly go forward, that our obedience to the beckonings of Providence may be the connecting link in the chain of occurrences which is to secure His purposes. The post occupied by Esther was not one of her seeking; the orderings of God's providence had placed her in that palace. Beyond the foresight of all who had brought about this elevation, a critical juncture had now occurred in the history of her people; and the very afforded opportunity of bringing relief to God's people, seemed to single her out as the proper actor in the case; and might justly encourage the belief that God designed through her to accomplish his purposes. So Mordecai looked at it; so Esther learned to see it; and the result proved that their duty and the designs of the Most High had been rightly interpreted.

But God has never changed any of the principles of his providential government; and here is a lesson of far wider application. We, who have the same God to serve, the same Providence to watch, may look upon this scene in the life of Esther, and learn the duty that belongs to us. By faithfully discerning the duty which Providence sets before us, and fully consecrating ourselves to its discharge, we may properly look for Divine protection and deliverance in danger, and for success in our aims. There is an important sense in which our lot and exact position in the church and in the world are as truly through the orderings of God's providence, as the elevation of Esther to that queenly throne. It is true of every one of us, that the circumstances about us are not entirely of our choosing, and that we are not living as we expected to live. The same Providence that ordered Esther's lot has ordered ours; and the same reasoning that influenced her, may be applied to us. The doctrine of providence, as taught in the Scriptures, applies not alone to queens and their stations—to nations and their exigencies—to the entire church of God and the dangers that threaten her; but the affairs of every man—especially of every believer in Christ—in every position in life, and at every moment of duty or pleasure, are ordered by Providence. No larger or more minute control can even be imagined, than that claimed by the Scriptural doctrine upon this subject. The sparrow cannot fall unregarded by His care; the lily cannot bloom without the colouring of his unrivalled pencil; not even a hair can fall from man's head that the eye of the Father sees not. The orderings of God have settled the age, the land, and the family, where each of us should be born; and our civil and religious advantages and opportunities. God's providence settles each pastor over a Christian church; determines who shall be his regular, and even who his occasional hearers; and the particular topic of discourse and the peculiar trains of thought in it, have often a providential adaptation to the necessities of the hearers far beyond the knowledge of the preacher. We are as truly a part of the Divine plan of providence as Esther was. Our voluntary agency may change our place in life; and we may disobey the providential calls of duty, as we shall see presently. But with all that we can do to order our own affairs, so much of things within us and around us, is ordered for us and beyond our control, that we may adopt for ourselves the principle Mordecai here suggests. Every opportunity of doing and getting good is to be carefully improved; and Providence calls us to embrace the advantages and to do the duties, which Providence sets before us.

Many important duties of the Christian life illustrate this great principle. God has given us our birth in an age, when we can do much to spread abroad his gospel. If we had been born one or two hundred years ago, our opportunities would have been far less favourable for sending the gospel to India or China. There were no Missionary Societies; no translated Bible; no awakened interest in the church upon the subject. The ability now to do this work, which God has promised shall be done, is a providential call to engage earnestly in it; and faith may believe that we are "brought to the kingdom for such a time as this." Let Christians make zealous efforts to save souls around them. The faithful presentation of truth to the heart and conscience, is God's appointed means of leading sinners to Christ. The efficacy is of God; but the means we are to use. Let us see to our duty. We are weak; therefore like Esther let us draw near to God in preparatory devotion, and rely upon his power. We are ignorant, and know not whom God will lead to salvation. But we know that the Redeemer shall see of the travail of his soul *and be satisfied;* Isa. liii. 11; and that all whom the Father hath given him shall come to him. The result is certain and our duty plain. Who knoweth but that a few kind, faithful words from your lips may form the connecting link of that chain of Providence—that chain of saving grace with which Providence coöperates—which shall draw upward an immortal soul to an everlasting salvation? Let faith watch for providential opportunities; for he that winneth souls is wise; and "they that turn many to righteousness shall shine as the stars for ever and ever."

And Mordecai's principle applies equally to our opportunities for getting good. You have an immortal soul, whose interests you are too prone to neglect. God gives you precious opportunities to secure its salvation. His providence has ordered your lot in this land. Here the sanctuary unfolds its inviting doors; here the Bible opens its instructive pages; here you have clear teachings of your sinfulness and exposure to wrath; and here the methods of his recovering grace are set before you. He calls and warns and invites and urges you to secure salvation. These very opportunities are providential indications of duty—providential encouragements of faith and effort. God gives you these opportunities. He has led you to hear these present teachings; he calls you now by the preacher's voice, to submit to Christ. Lift up your heart now to him; he calls you to be saved. You are better off than Esther; for the promise comes to you without a peradventure. "Whosoever shall call upon the name of the Lord shall be saved!" Rom. x. 13. Oh, important crisis in the history of an immortal being! Who knoweth whether thou art come to the sanctuary, for such a time, for such an event as this?

"He that watches for providences," said an eminent servant of God, "will have enough of providences to watch." God blesses the souls of those men who carefully watch his designs, and earnestly endeavour to promote them. We *must* watch how God works in order to know what he calls upon us to do. And if we are careless of the lessons of God's providence, or of the just interpretation of them according to the light thrown upon our duty by the word of God, we cast ourselves out of the Divine protection, and reject his eternal counsels against our own souls.

But this leads us to consider a fourth principle of great importance implied in the words of Mordecai to Esther. He contemplates it as a possibility, that she may refuse to do her duty in this important crisis, and virtually asks the question, Will this defeat the settled purposes of God? Notice here, my brethren, that the drift of this passage cuts up by the roots the usual objection that the sovereign and settled purposes of God come into collision with the free agency of men. We believe, through the teachings of the word and of Providence, that God has his eternal purposes; and that these are so carried out as to leave man free. Here then arises the question, Suppose that any man refuses to do his duty, shall God's purposes fail? Is it possible for man's neglect or disobedience to thwart the purposes of God? By no means. Mordecai is certain that God will bring deliverance to his people; and yet he contemplates the possibility of Esther's unfaithfulness. In that event he warns her of two results: first, enlargement and deliverance shall arise from some other quarter; second, she and her house shall be destroyed. Here is an important lesson indeed. Men may destroy their own souls by unfaithfulness in duty; but they cannot thwart the purposes of God. He will never lack agents to execute his designs; and the only effect of a sinner's folly and wickedness will be his own destruction. The great designs of Providence will move on; we cannot stay them; and if we urge not forward the triumphs of the Divine government, we shall be trodden down and crushed in its onward march.

It is perilous for the Christian church to falter, to be negligent, to be disobedient to the beckonings of Providence, when she is called to earnest zeal. We dare not draw back. However difficult the duty, or delicate or responsible, we must go forward. Hardly any expression is more worthy of our deep pondering than this of Mordecai, FOR SUCH A TIME AS THIS. Let us watch for duties and seize the time, lest our golden opportunities hurry by our laggard footsteps, and leave us beyond remedy to mourn and perish. God will not wait on our loitering. See Israel scattered, rejected, and wretched, because they knew not the time of their visitation. See the churches planted by the labours of the Apostles; the candlestick has been removed. Our only safety is in earnest faith and diligent obedience. Let these motives address our faith, and our fears, and our hopes. 1st, God will certainly accomplish all his purposes: 2d, If we refuse to do them, he will find other instruments: 3d, Our neglect or disobedience will be our own destruction: and 4th, We should watch and obey his providential indications of duty.

You may refuse, at such a time as this, to aid in prosecuting the cause of missions, by which the command and the providence of God now urge you to bless a dying world; you are at liberty to refuse; but that cause will go on. God has certainly purposed it; he will find other hearts more willing, and other hands more liberal; and he will punish you for refusing to obey his beckoning. You may neglect your duty to souls around you; the Redeemer's work shall be done; and your apathy and disobedience shall meet their reward. Esther durst not disobey, even in the palace; nor may any man in the church of God. Indeed she was brought to the palace for such a time and for this very duty; and your place in the church of Christ is assigned to you for the very purpose of honouring Christ, as his word and the time set your duties before you.

Let every impenitent soul feel the warnings and the encouragements of these weighty thoughts. God gives you precious opportunities for securing your salvation; he gives you advantages, which thousands never had; he has led you now to the sanctuary and urges you to forsake sin; he bids you remember *the time;* he calls you to "flee from the wrath to come." In his name, I exhort you, as Mordecai exhorted Esther, to consider the greatest duty of your mortal life—even the securing of an immortal one. Consider these favourable indications of God's providence as the gracious foreshadowing of his willingness to pardon. Be very certain of this, that God will never bring you into his kingdom of grace or glory, against your own consent. He will never save you without first converting you. Seek then his converting grace; and use those means which God blesses for the salvation of sinners. Come seriously to the Bible to learn his will; bow down humbly at the mercy-seat to ask his favour; draw near to Jesus and choose him as your Master. To these things you are now invited. Give your heart now to Christ. Possibly, however, these teachings excite no interest in you; possibly they excite bitter enmity. This is your folly; and may be your destruction. You may refuse Jesus and his salvation now; you may refuse for ever. That refusal cannot rob the Redeemer of a single jewel in his glorious crown. You cannot thwart him. He will fill up the mansions of glory in spite of your neglect or opposition. But you bring destruction upon your own soul. Think of this; and refuse not now the call of mercy. These very thoughts make this opportunity of hearing the gospel, more solemn and important. Put not away from you everlasting life. "To-day if ye will hear his voice, harden not your hearts." Ps. xcv. 7, 8. Determine now to be for Christ. Say, now, with the Persian queen, I will go in unto the King. Take this Bible as your guide; this Saviour, as your Saviour; Choose God's people as your companions; make his service your delight. Who knoweth but you have been led to hear these very truths; to enjoy this season of worship; that you may cheerfully embrace the gracious indications of God's providence, give your soul to the Redeemer, and be saved?

LECTURE VI.

ESTHER'S NOBLE RESOLVE.

THE earnest argument of Mordecai was not lost upon Esther. If previously she had any wavering of purpose, as she feared for her acceptance before her husband, and despaired of being able to succour her people; she now no longer has any hesitation, either with reference to the path in which her duty urged her; or in reference to her own immediate obedience to the promptings of duty. She has made up her mind. She could not know how she would be received; she had the same reasons to fear as when she first replied to Mordecai; she could not put down the apprehension that the issue might be her own destruction. She resolved to go before Ahasuerus—and she resolved wisely. Every wise decision is made in view of both sides of the question. Before the mind of Esther rose all the difficulties she could not overlook; but before her rose also the urgent necessities she could not but feel. And the balance was turned by the promptings of faith in the covenant of her God. It seemed like madly rushing upon death to venture unbidden before the king; it seemed like tempting the providence of God to her sure destruction, if she neglected the favourable juncture of duty; and faith urged that the opportunity now offered to secure an important blessing. And it is plain to us now, that Esther made a reasonable choice. She might perish, but with a clear conscience, if she made the venture; she would certainly perish, so Mordecai urged, if she neglected this effort. And it seems strange indeed that men generally do not more fully and frequently recognize the truth, that there is less responsibility in doing our duty, than there is in evading it; that daring as Esther's resolution may justly be thought, she would have been more wickedly daring, if she had resisted her duty and turned from the expostulations of Mordecai. Now she exposes her mortal life to the possible anger of Ahasuerus; but had she made no effort to relieve her people, she would have exposed her soul to the certain anger of a greater King—the Ruler and Protector of Israel!

But it is not the tendency of piety, or of its principles, to set us free from the wise restraints of prudence, nor to encourage the careless performance of any duty. Genuine faith differs widely from a presumptuous confidence, not only as founded upon better evidences, but as exerting a different and more salutary influence upon ourselves. Presumption is bold, even to insolence; and venturesome, because fearless. True faith, on the contrary, is keen-sighted to discern the real difficulties before us and around us; it is therefore cautious; and while not undervaluing difficulties, exhibits its true strength by meeting and overcoming fears and obstacles. Faith prompts the most careful and judicious measures to secure the end we seek; and walks on the line between the extremes of despondency, that deems all exertion useless, and presumption, that deems exertion needless. And here is the truthfulness of this narrative to human experience. Had many a human writer penned this history, we would have read of Esther's boldness to secure the desired relief; rising up immediately at the suggestion of Mordecai, and proceeding at once to the unbidden presence of the king. But it is far otherwise here; and the lesson here taught is more faithful to nature.

Two matters here exhibit the queen's prudence:

First, As becomes a pious woman, Esther uses means to secure the special favour and blessing of God upon her momentous enterprise. No pious mind should be willing to engage in any duty upon which first the blessing of God is not sought; much less will such a mind engage in any responsible and important enterprise in a thoughtless manner. You remember we noticed that the name of God does not occur in this book. But it must be acknowledged, that a solemn service of this kind is a plain recognition of the Divine existence and of the Divine rule. Esther teaches us here, that engagements of peculiar importance demand special exercises of devotion. Fasting is an extraordinary means of grace. It is to be made use of—never in the light of a penance, the Bible nowhere enjoins penance; much as it says of penitence—in token of our humiliation before God; when we anticipate a threatening evil, or mourn under chastisement, or lament our deep unfaithfulness, or undertake a duty which calls for special Divine strengthening. The distress and peril of the Jews through the success of their foe, Haman, have called Esther to this perilous duty; her hope is to avert the calamity; and to fast is the appropriate symbol of her humiliation before the Lord. The fastings spoken of in Scripture do not always imply a rigorous abstinence from all food. The prophet Daniel fasted three full weeks: he ate no pleasant bread, neither did flesh nor wine come into his mouth. Dan. x. 2, 3. Though brief fastings might imply an entire abstinence from food, longer seasons were not so kept. Daniel ate for the support of nature; but refrained from the delights of the table. Thus we suppose the fast of Esther was kept for three days. The luxurious viands spread for the queen of Persia lie untasted before her; her earnest anxieties are awakened for her people; and her soul is humbled before her God. Her maidens were associated with her in this solemn duty. The pious Esther had perhaps gathered about her as maids of honour to the queen, a band of the daughters of Israel; or perhaps her quiet but earnest zeal for the faith of her fathers and for the glory of her covenant God, had led her to teach those immediately under her control the name of Israel's Lord. Perhaps among no other heathen nation could Esther have kept secret her nation and her religion, so well as among the Persians. For they were like the Jews of the dispersion in this, that they worshipped without either temples or images; and therefore the external difference between the Jew and the Persian was less striking. Yet if Esther had thus gathered about her a band of Jewish damsels, we can easily see that her faith was not an entire secret in the palace, so that the danger which Mordecai pointed out was greater: "Think not with thyself that thou shalt escape in the king's house." One Jewess, and she the queen, might possibly escape the execution of the edict; but a band of females adoring Jehovah in the very palace, could scarcely expect exemption though the queen stood among them. But it sets the piety of Esther before us in a favourable light, that she was surrounded by maidens who were ready to join with her in her devotions. Circumstances may throw even a good man into bad company, and his duty may detain him there; but the man who has it in his power to choose his company, and is then found with the idle, the frivolous, or the wicked, may justly be judged, as to his own character, by the company he keeps.

Judge a man by the books he loves to read, and by the associates he cherishes.

But Esther desired also that the prayers and humiliation of God's people should be joined to the supplications in the palace for the success of her important enterprise. So she urged Mordecai to gather the Jews in Shushan that they also might fast. If they neither ate nor drank literally, it is likely that the three days were reckoned according to Jewish custom: two nights and the intervening day. Thus our Lord lay three days in the grave; being buried on our Friday evening and rising on Sabbath morning very early. This view is strengthened by the fact that Esther went in to the king on the third day. In thus associating the Jews with her in this solemn duty, Esther teaches us her estimate of the prayers of the brethren, and urges us to desire an interest in their intercessions. For our God is the hearer of prayer.

Having thus sought God's blessing, Esther, in the second place, used due means to win the favour of her royal husband.

She teaches us the right order: God's favour first, man's next. But while man's favour is subordinate always, a pious regard to God's will does not allow us to disregard the means of reaching and influencing our fellow-men. That is a spurious independence, which is reckless of the views and opinions of the world around. Dependence on God is entirely consistent with wise efforts to influence men about us. "I am made all things to all men," is the expression of an earnest Apostle, who yet affords us in his character, a righteous independence with regard to man, and an entire dependence for all his success upon the power of God. Esther rises from fastings and prayer, and makes such preparations as seem adapted to touch favourably the heart of the king. We may judge from the preceding narrative, that she was a woman of great personal beauty; and it is well known that in all ages elegance of person has been rather characteristic of the Jewish female. And now the budding rose that a few years since had been transplanted from the nursery of Mordecai to the royal garden, has expanded into the full blown blooming of a stately matron; to a husband's eye, a riper and more captivating style of beauty. To heighten the impression, the queen arrayed herself in the magnificent robes of her station; threw perhaps over her shoulders a mantle which *he* had admired; and placed in her hair a brilliant ornament, chiefly prized as *his* gift. She knew how much depended upon touching a tender chord in the bosom of her husband.

The Bible says very little to excite, and nothing to commend, the vanity of our race, in male or female. If the object of Esther had been merely the adorning of her beautiful person, and while thus arrayed in purple and precious stones, she had lacked the nobler ornament of a pious and believing spirit; then we would find no approbation here of her royal robes. But in truth, the outward adorning is a matter of but small importance, if the heart is truly right; and the dress may be more or less costly, according to the worldly circumstances of the wearer. On the one hand, she should not be proud, who has nothing to adorn her but her dress; and on the other hand, we can easily know that pride may scoff at silks, as well as wear them. Never before perhaps had Esther been so careful in the arrangement of her toilette; yet her heart was fixed, not upon her dress, but upon the great object she used these means to secure. If personal vanity had as little usually to do with the adorning of even pious females, we would need fewer cautions upon the subject of extravagance; we would see larger attention given to improved minds and cultivated affections; and happy hearts everywhere would make happy homes. Then would our "daughters be as corner stones, polished after the similitude of a palace." Ps. cxliv. 12.

Behold now the intrepid yet the trembling Esther clothed in royal apparel and about to venture in to the king! It requires far more calm and deliberate courage to move forward into a great peril in this way, than it does to rush into the excitement and strife of a battle. There is every reason to judge that the conflicts in Esther's mind were those we too would have felt in a case of so great importance; where the issue is unknown; and where we cannot but fear that it may be adverse. On the one hand, fear of the king depressed her; on the other, hopes of divine aid and deliverance buoyed her up. These peculiar alternations of hope and fear, we doubtless have all felt. But faith bore her forward. Esther feared, for she was human; but be it recorded to her praise, she did not falter. She has left now the apartments of the women, and perhaps her attendants weeping, as they forecast her fate; and has passed to the king's sanctuary. The frowning guards, that kept the door where she was to enter, start up in amazement at the strange sight of a queenly, yet an unbidden suppliant at that proud throne, whence Vashti had been so rudely thrust down; and held their breath with sympathetic terror, as the beautiful petitioner passed on perhaps to meet her death. The executioner of the royal mandates, ever prepared for his work of blood, stood ready with half drawn scimetar to carry out the stern decree of Persian law. The eye of Esther took all this in at a glance; and her heart, ah! it had been soothed to calmness in the presence of her God; and faith in Israel's covenant held back a woman's fears. The dread portal is passed; and the eye of Ahasuerus is upon her. Is he her husband, or her judge? her deliverer, or her executioner? Will the golden sceptre move? Or will the stern eye of the despot gaze coldly upon his unbidden guest? What a moment of solemn expectancy! Not for Esther's fate alone! That was a small matter. The decree for death to a woman acting such a part, would but have dismissed her from a marble to a golden palace; from an earthly to a heavenly crown. But upon the lips of Ahasuerus trembles the fate of her people. The crisis is come, and past! The smile of the king assures her; he reaches forth his golden sceptre. ESTHER IS WELCOME AND ISRAEL IS SAFE!

The king held out the golden sceptre; and the queen drew near, and touched the top of it. Thus her life was safe; but she had not yet accomplished her errand. She felt however assured that her nation was unsuspected; and that she was not included in the dreadful decree; and this perhaps formed the basis of her further proceedings. The king stops not with granting her her life. His gracious words are, "What wilt thou, queen Esther, and what is thy request? It shall be even given thee to the half of the kingdom." But how strange appears to us the termination of this important errand! Esther had sought this interview to ask the life of her people, and their deliverance from the malice of Haman; and yet her request seems to be a new favour upon the haughty favourite. She simply asks that Haman may be invited with the king, to partake with her of a banquet of wine; and when at this banquet, the king again affords her an opportunity for a large petition, she renews her request, that these two guests may again be present on the next day, upon a like occasion. Why does Esther delay thus to urge that great request which weighs so heavily upon her heart? Especially, why does she substitute what seems a favour to Haman, while yet she aims at the overthrow of all his schemes?

It is possible, Esther was too much agitated to present her request that day before the king. In the prospect of some great duty, we brace ourselves to its performance; but when the crisis is past, the excitement dies, and we are all unnerved. Esther had suddenly passed from extreme anxiety to joy unbounded; and her feelings, controlled by too great an effort, would not allow her, during that day, to venture further. She must gain entire composure before she can plead so great a cause. But she may have been influenced, also, by a prudent policy. She desired to make the proper impression, and to embrace the fitting time in reference to three parties upon this great occasion.

First. In the most effectual way, she wished to secure the king's favour, and to lead him to engage himself voluntarily upon her side. In the court, and while he sat upon that stately throne, surrounded by the fearful tokens of her recent peril, the time and place were not so fit to plead, nor even to mention such a matter. She was about to accuse a man upon whom the king had lavished his highest honours; she was indeed about tacitly to censure the king himself for the folly and even the wickedness that had signed so thoughtlessly that fatal decree—and it became her to move cautiously.

But *secondly*, it was a master-stroke of policy

that included Haman in the invitation to the banquet. It threw that wily minister completely off his guard, and prevented him from plotting any schemes to counteract the queen's designs. Knowing, as she did, both the king and his minister, she played with the pride of the one, while she prepared to awaken the king's anger, and have it consummate its purpose by the presence of its guilty object.

And *thirdly*, by this course she wished effectually to turn the minds of the Jewish people away from herself, as the instrument of deliverance, and fix them upon God, the great Deliverer. The Jews of the city had formed high expectations concerning Esther's interview with the king. They had prayed, with solemn fasting, for her success; and yet if her success had been immediate, they would have been too much disposed to glorify the queen as the author of it. It may have been with feelings of bitter disappointment, that they heard of her request for Haman's presence at her banquet of wine; so little do men know of the wise plans which work their surest good. But if their disappointment drove them again to depend upon God, they would be better prepared to recognize his hand in the final result.

But doubtless, the restraining influence of God's providence led Esther to these first requests. The motives we suggest, were the agencies to effect His purposes; and other matters must be introduced into the history before all is ready for Haman's disgrace and destruction. We may not know God's restraining finger to keep us from evil, or to delay a coming good; "but he that believeth shall not make haste," Isaiah xxviii. 16. Let the pious mind roll its care upon God. What he does and what he omits to do, shall work for good. As Esther invoked the Divine blessing, we may believe that Divine restraint influenced her modest requests.

But while we wait the movements of Providence, which for a little season leave Esther out of sight, let us learn from the scenes in this lecture, how we may discharge those important duties of our own lives, where it is often impossible to decide which is greatest—the fear to act, or the necessity to act; for such perplexing responsibilities occur, every now and then, in all our paths through life.

Christians are often placed in circumstances of deep perplexity. They seem forsaken of God. Their enemies laugh; their fears rise; their sins prevail. Learn, 1st. These are no strange trials. God appoints them to prove his people. Perhaps never a man lived a Christian life without passing through many seasons of difficulty and perplexity. It is the province of faith to support us in such times. Faith is reliance upon the truth of God, and its clearest proof is seen in times of severest trial. A coin that counterfeits gold may escape detection when tested by a weak acid, and may not melt in an ordinary fire; but pure gold will abide the action of the strongest acids, and be only brighter in the hottest crucible. Would you look upon some dark scenes in religious experience, and see God apparently deserting his people? Read your Bible. Recall those trying three days, when Abraham journeyed to Moriah with his beloved Isaac, mourning for his son, fearing ever again to look his bereaved Sarah in the face, yet firmly resolved to do his Lord's bidding. Forget not Esther's three days' fasting in anxious uncertainty for the issue of her petition. Remember those three days—most remarkable in the history of the world—when the Lord of glory lay in the sepulchre of Joseph, when his apostles were dispirited, and hardly hoped and believed enough to keep them from scattering, and to lead them on the third morning to the tomb where Jesus had lain. Trouble is no new thing in the ways of piety. Then, learn, 2d. Trials are not desertions. They prove our faith; they awaken our gratitude; they quicken our love; they show the Lord's loving-kindness. We can easily see that it was better for Abraham; better for Esther; better for the apostles of Christ, that they passed through these trials. We see that our brethren are holier and more useful after severe discipline; and why should we not judge our own trials designed for good? Learn, 3d, our duty. We are not to trust appearances, nor judge the frowns of Providence proofs that we are cast off, nor shrink from the path of right. We may have our fears. This is natural; but we must not yield to fear. We should use all proper means to find relief. So Esther prays for divine aid, and propitiates the king.

But, especially, we should make the bold ventures of faith. Let us argue that when matters are darkest, faith is still reasonable. We have surely nothing to gain by desponding. If we cannot look to God, we cannot look elsewhere; but we may look to God in the darkest hour. When our eye cannot penetrate the darkness, and even faith can see but one step in advance, let us take that step. The darkness of a path of duty is not so dreadful as the despair in every other path. If shut up, like Esther, to say, "If I perish, I perish; if I must die, let it be in the effort of duty." If we may say, "Better die doing right, than live doing wrong," how much more, "Better die trusting God than perish beneath his curse through despair of his mercy!"

Sinful men, who have never fled to Christ for salvation, and lie beneath the curse of a broken law, should learn a most important lesson from Esther.

She and her people were exposed to destruction. The condition of every impenitent soul is unspeakably more serious and dreadful. The decree of a King more mighty, more just, and more inflexible has gone forth. God's voice cries, "The soul that sinneth it shall die." Ezek. xviii. 4. At the worst Ahasuerus could kill the body; but we may "fear Him who after he has killed has power to destroy both soul and body in hell." Matt. x. 28. The edict of Persia was nominally unalterable; God's law is really unchangeable; that decree was unjust, but the sinner is condemned by a righteous sentence. If Mordecai wept, and Esther fasted, and the Jews lay in sackcloth; well may every sinner fear for the wrath of God against him. Let your deep personal responsibility lead you to ponder Esther's example, and flee from the wrath to come.

Esther hoped for deliverance through the favour of the king. The sinner can expect safety and deliverance only through the sovereign mercy of God. The king sat on his throne, and held in his hand a golden sceptre. If he refused to hold it forth, the boldest petitioner must die. Our sovereign King sits upon a throne of grace, and the touch of his golden sceptre secures the immortal life of the priceless soul. If he touches us not, we die. We are truly dependent upon the grace of Christ—and the issue is infinitely more important than when Esther drew near the Persian throne. It is reasonable, if we would secure eternal life, that we should bow at the throne of grace, and ask for it.

Nor does the sinful soul lack fears and hopes, perplexing thoughts and urgent arguments, akin to those of Esther. She flattered herself, as sinful men are prone to do. But Mordecai's faithful expostulation urged her to find safety in the path of duty. The queen in the palace must not neglect her people; and no sinner, in the church or elsewhere, can secure his soul's salvation, unless he goes boldly forward in his most important duty—to bow submissively before a sovereign God! Esther feared also. The king might not receive her. Already her name, perhaps, was written upon the dark list, especially proscribed in Haman's fierce revenge; she had not seen her lord's face for many days; she was unbidden to his presence. With many tremblings she resolved to go; and doubtless was driven at last by the well pondered reflection, that here only was safety. A faithful voice rung in her ears, to stay away was but to perish. It seemed a desperate undertaking whichever way she turned; but her only hope was in resolving, "I will go in to the king." Perhaps he might extend to her the golden sceptre for her life and the safety of her people. If he did not, she must die; yet even then there would be a satisfaction in dying in the virtuous effort to deliver Israel.

The position and resolution of Esther may remind us of a similar remarkable resolution recorded in the Bible. Just such a desperate case; just such a decision; and just such a gracious deliverance occurred long before in Israelitish history. 2 Kings vii. 3, &c. The city of Samaria was closely besieged in the time of Ahab; the provisions were exhausted; famine reigned in the streets; and the destruction of the city seemed near at hand. One eventful evening as the shadows of twilight were gathering over the land, there sat four leprous men in the gate of the besieged city, at the point of starving, and reasoning with themselves on the folly of making no earnest effort to save their wretched lives. Why sit we here, said they, until we die? Ours is a desperate case. If we sit here we die; if we enter into the miserable city, the strong and needed warriors are perishing there for hunger, and they have nothing to spare for lepers, unclean in person and unfit to fight; if we go forth to the enemy, it is very likely they will put us to death. They might take healthy men prisoners; but in all likelihood they will kill lepers. But it is our only hope. Desperate though it seems, every other hope is cut off. They may kill us—but we must die if we do not go. And they may spare our lives! Our very wretchedness may appeal to them; and we may live. These men acted upon this desperate resolve; and lo! God had interposed for the deliverance of Samaria. They not only saved their own lives, but brought plenty into the city, and rejoicing to their people.

When sinful men begin to awake to their true condition before the holy law of God, they are often in deep and painful perplexity, such as these instances describe. Let every such soul use this wise reasoning, respecting its salvation. Every sinful soul must perish, unless Christ Jesus has mercy upon it, and extends the golden sceptre of his renewing grace. Lay aside the flatteries, which delay or prevent your earnest approach to the throne of grace;

for they are delusive. Listen not to your fears, though they are many and greatly distress you. You may think God has recorded your name for destruction; you may feel that you are not bidden to approach; you may tremble lest your day of grace is past, and it is in vain to pray; you may even say, I have felt; I have wept; I have prayed; and it is all in vain for me to approach to God. Sinful soul, make the very worst of your case. Know the very worst, if you can, of your sins; imagine the worst of the hardness of your heart and of God's unwillingness to save; and the stronger you make the difficulties preventing your salvation, and the more unlikely it seems that a righteous God will have mercy on your soul the more urgent are the reasons for giving your immediate attention to the concerns of religion, and for pressing at once to the footstool of Divine mercy. IT IS YOUR ONLY HOPE! You perish certainly, if you neglect salvation; and you can but perish, if you give it your earnest attention. There never can be a good reason for any sinner's neglecting his salvation; there never can be a good reason for a living sinner ceasing to implore God's pardoning grace. Even the certainty that God will not hear some, is no good reason; for no man can certainly know that this is his case. If the heart is hard, refusing or neglecting to pray will make it no softer; if your sins are many now in number, to neglect the mercy-seat will but tend to swell the number; if there is danger that even already the Lord will not forgive, that danger increases the longer you go on in sin. It may be a place of deep solemnity, and a time of deep responsibility, to go alone before your God, and plead earnestly for the salvation of your sinful soul; as it was deeply solemn for Esther to venture before the king. But it was folly and responsibility unspeakably greater for her to shrink from this duty. God's people would have found deliverance otherwise, while she would have perished. And so may every sinner judge of his own case. It is a serious thing to be an anxious sinner; it is inexpressibly more serious to be a careless sinner. It is a solemn thing to plead before God for your soul's salvation; it is infinitely more solemn to be under his wrath and curse, and neglect such pleadings. No man can evade his responsibilities; you are shut up to the choice of one solemn thing or another—to perish in your sins, or to make an earnest effort to secure eternal life.

Thus before every impenitent soul is substantially a choice like this of Esther's, yet of infinitely greater personal inducements. When you have made the very worst of your own condition, if disposed to fear, and to argue despondingly; when you fear most that God will not hear; when you judge yourself wholly unbidden to approach the mercy-seat, your case is no worse than hers; and the resolution is a wise one, "I will go in to the king; and if I perish, I perish."

But while we argue the matter thus with the fears

of sinful men, we are not willing to allow that full justice is done to the calls of the gospel of grace by this view of the subject. Ye all, who have souls defiled with sin, and are urged by the invitations of mercy to come to the great and healing fountain of a Saviour's blood, are in circumstances far more hopeful than the Persian queen. She came in before a capricious tyrant; and you come before a gracious God. She understood not how an unalterable decree of Persia could be set aside; she feared it was impossible; and we may know how God's law, while yet unchanging, is magnified and satisfied by the sacrifice of Calvary. She came unbidden and without a word of encouragement to that throne, whence many had been cast down; and though our fears often place us upon a level with her, yet against such fears should we still press on; or better than this, our faith should lay hold upon the many commands and solicitations and promises of God's holy word, which are extended to every humble soul, and on which we are fully warranted to rely. She came to plead for Israel's temporal deliverance; we come to plead for the soul's life.

Look at it any way you will, and the sinner should flee to Jesus. If you are not as deeply affected by your sins as you are conscious you should be, yet come to Jesus, for he gives repentance. If he seems not to hear or even to spurn you, so did he to an humble woman once in the days of his flesh, whom yet he received and blessed. Matt. xv. 21—

28. Your path though dark is not a strange one; many a saved sinner has trodden it before. Your difficulties though numerous are just such difficulties as others have passed through and touched the golden sceptre. Let not your perplexities and fears cause you to lose sight of the necessities yet deeper, which urge you on. Your sins may be many. Not a doubt, but that they are greater than you think for. You have no claims upon mercy long abused. This is very true. But while pondering your difficulties choose not the very worst. The worst thing you can do is to turn your back on Christ—the only Redeemer. You must perish, if you are unbelieving; you must perish, if you are hardened; you must perish, if you are careless; you must perish, if you neglect the great salvation! You can but be rejected, if you fly to Christ. Resolve that you will go to Jesus. Christ never rejected any. His own word is, "Him that cometh unto me I will IN NO WISE cast out." John vi. 37. Resolve that you will be the first one rejected, if you are not received. Your eternal life is at stake. Drive away your fears. Fly to Jesus. Be in haste lest you be too late!

Come humble sinner in whose breast
A thousand thoughts revolve;
Come with your grief and fears opprest
And make this last resolve.
I'll go to Jesus, though my sin,
High as a mountain rose;
I know his courts, I'll enter in,
Whatever may oppose.

Prostrate I'll lie before his throne,
And there my guilt confess :
I'll tell him I'm a wretch undone
Without his sovereign grace.
I'll to the gracious King approach
Whose sceptre pardon gives :
Perhaps he may command my touch,
And then the suppliant lives.

Perhaps he will admit my plea,
Perhaps will hear my prayer ;
But if I perish I will pray,
And perish only there.
I can but perish if I go,
I am resolved to try ;
For if I stay away, I know
I must for ever die.

LECTURE VII.

THE SLEEPLESS NIGHT.

THE unfinished plans of Esther we may not further pursue, till we delay to trace the strange workings of Providence in preparing for their complete success. Within the compass of a few verses, we may see the eventful changes of human life. Who knoweth indeed what a day may bring forth? "The Lord maketh poor and maketh rich; he bringeth low and lifteth up." 1 Sam. ii. 7.

The first proud step that passes before us is that of Haman "joyful and with a glad heart." Added to all the honours heretofore enjoyed in the realm of Persia by Haman the Magnificent, a new one had that day been granted from a most unexpected quarter; and perhaps his vain and conceited mind imagined himself beginning a new career of preferment. So far as Esther has designed by her attention to the favourite, either to conciliate the king, or to throw the wily Agagite off his guard, she has completely succeeded. The new honour swells his heart with new pride, and no suspicions of evil enter his mind.

It may seem a strange thing to us in the abstract

reflection, that in a world so completely governed by a righteous God, wicked men can be joyful and glad of heart. Yet we see it all around us; we find it fully recognized in the sacred Scriptures, that there are pleasures in sin; and the joy of the wicked in their prosperity has distressed and grieved many a dejected believer. So a Psalmist writes, "My feet had almost gone; my steps had well nigh slipped; I was envious at the foolish, when I saw the prosperity of the wicked." Psalm lxxiii. 2, 3. These things are a part of the wonderful dealings of His hand, who tries the hearts of the children of men. So we need not grieve while such men as Haman pass before us in the joy of their hearts. Nor let us embrace the fallacy of supposing that since Haman was not a Jew, we may justify his hatred to the Israel of God; or that the long cherished enmity between Israel and Amalek was any proper reason for his continued hostility. We may thus account for Haman's feelings and conduct; but to explain a matter of this kind is not to justify it. It is not from the circumstances of a man, it is from his very nature that he is under obligations to love and obey God. No matter in what family, or nation, or church a man may be born; no matter what his education or prejudices; no matter whether he is willing or unwilling: so far as right is concerned, he is bound by all the laws of God; bound to practise justice and speak the truth; bound to love his neighbour as himself;

bound to obey every dictate of righteousness; bound to glorify God "in his body and spirit." The people of Haman were rebels against the God of Israel; they had fought against his people; and it is not wonderful that Haman identified himself in the pride of an unrighteous heart, with the unrighteous cause of an unrighteous people. And there are not wanting men who in our own age will support their nation, their party, or their church in wrong, as firmly as in right. This no righteous man can ever do. That my nation is wrong in any matter, may be no reason why I should turn my hand against my people; but it is a reason why I should refuse to give my support to that which is wrong. If the church in which I was born, is erroneous in doctrine, or corrupt in practice, it is vastly more important that I should be faithful to God's truth, than to any organization that is set in array against him. It is utterly inconsistent with the principles of righteousness to judge, that every man should continue to hold the sentiments with which he was educated. Amidst the jarring ideas of the world, many must be wrong; and improvement implies change. Every change towards truth and righteousness is wise; and our responsibilities lie in this, that we should make our changes in obedience to an intelligent conscience, and not at the promptings of impulse, or at the solicitations of vice. Long continuance in iniquity—education in iniquity, can afford no adequate apology for ungodliness.

Yet there are not wanting men, who resolve to live and die as their fathers have done, even though the light of God's serious truth convinces them that their fathers were wrong. There are not wanting men, who would plead as an excuse, nay, as some justification for disregarding Jehovah and transgressing his commands, that they are not members of the church; and perhaps that their fathers were not before them. The reasoning is as wicked as it is impotent. Apply it to Satan, and you would make him sinless before the judgment seat of God, and an undeserving sufferer in chains of darkness. For, no long array of generations in human life can stretch so far back as the rebellion of the first apostate; and no fighting against the church of God can exceed his malevolence. If Satan is not sinless, though long and thoroughly ungodly, any man is wicked who stands off from the truth and the church of God; or sets himself in opposition to Jehovah. Hear ye this, all ye sons of men! Woe, on the one hand, to that ungodly child of a pious parentage, who breaks the covenant of God that has descended to him through a long line of those that loved and served the Lord; that breaks down in his household that altar of piety whence the flame of devotion has ascended for ages back; and that begins a new generation of the sons of Belial, trained without prayer and without the covenant seal of consecration upon them! And woe, on the other hand, to that man whose father and whose father's father were "aliens from the commonwealth of Israel and strangers to the covenants of promise." Eph. ii. 12; were careless of salvation and hardened in sin; who adopts and endorses the bad principles in which he was trained, refuses the wiser and holier teachings by which God would correct his ways, and trains up his household to a like and a more resolute ungodliness! The curses of a righteous God will smoke against such men; the fire of his anger will burn against them, all the more fiercely from the very thoroughness of their ungodliness. No sinner before His eye can be justified in iniquity. Haman is an enemy to God, and none the less so, that his royal line has been of consistent wickedness for many generations back.

And this man is joyful and glad of heart. How is this consistent with the declaration of the Scriptures, "The wicked are like the troubled sea which cannot rest, whose waters cast up mire and dirt; there is no peace, saith my God, to the wicked?" Isa. lvii. 20, 21.

Wait a moment and you may understand. Even the sea is not always "the troubled sea;" and you may gaze far down into the calm and pure waters, as if no mire could ever becloud their crystal clearness. The sea is the emblem of instability. A passing breeze disturbs that deceitful calm; and the swelling and turbid waters show their angry might. The peace of the wicked is like the sea; as deceitful, as unstable, and as dangerous in its stormy recoil. Another bold step—we will not say a proud, much less a haughty one—another step, firm and bold, advances in these scenes, to teach us how easily that deceitful joy in Haman's heart may change to the turbid swellings of hatred and malice. As Haman passed out of the palace, his eye fell on the impassionate form of Mordecai the Jew.

This, it may be, is their first meeting since the open understanding that they are mortal foes. And now surely that so important a matter is at issue between them; when even Esther the queen seems to show complaisance and policy enough to extend to the favourite an invitation to her banquet of wine; when it seems important that no new provocation be stirred up in the breast of so powerful a foe, surely now Mordecai will give some tokens of external respect; the lips that bewailed the edict with a cry so bitter, will speak one soft word, to mollify increasing wrath. At least Mordecai, having sufficiently wounded Haman's pride, may now step silently aside, and avoid aggravating the wound. But let not the standard of worldly policy be used in judging this high principled and manly Jew. "It is better to trust in the Lord than to put confidence in princes." Psa. cxviii. 9. We cast no reflections upon Esther's prudent policy, as if it implied less uprightness of character. Possibly Mordecai sees here a principle, which had not occurred to the queen in her apparent court to Haman; or we may have here an example of the differing judgments of even pious minds, touching the same things. Even deciding that Esther adopted no wrong policy, we may admire Mordecai's consistent firmness. "Mordecai stood not up nor did him reverence." His trust is fixed upon that God who can deliver; he asks no mercy from that man's hands from whom he would scorn to receive it; and he has no mark to show of a respect he does not feel, for the foe of his God and of his race.

"Then went Haman forth that day joyful and with a glad heart." But how shallow the joy of a wicked mind! how easily is it disturbed by trifles for which a good man would care nothing! As he passed forth from the palace he saw Mordecai the Jew. The sweet is turned to bitter; the gladness has become wretchedness; the muddy sediment at the bottom of his cup of earthly pleasure is stirred up, and the potion tastes like gall and wormwood. Look carefully at the principles here involved; for they govern widely the scenes of earth. Look at the contrasts between these two men; between their characters primarily; between their conduct and their enjoyments, as flowing from their characters; and learn that lesson of salutary wisdom from our Divine Teacher of far later days, "A man's life consisteth not in the abundance of the things which he possesseth." Luke xii. 15. We are not told how Mordecai felt at this casual interview; but we have no reason to suppose that with all his anxiety for the hastening issue, there was a single sting of that remorse, which poisons the current of vital joy in a mortal's veins. We know this much, that every intelligent mind would prefer to share the feelings of Mordecai, rather than those of Haman. The favourite of the king is deeply wretched. He hurried home, and in the presence of his wife and his confidential friends gave utterance to feelings, which may often dwell in the minds of wicked men; but which in the usages of our social manners, as compared with oriental customs, far less frequently among us, find utterance in language so explicit. He recounted in their ears, as an oriental would, his riches, his children, his honour; he told them of the new mark of respect, which he had that day received from Esther the queen; and then the lamentable confession is, after all, that these are empty baubles; that these coveted things of earth can afford no real happiness—" All this availeth me nothing so long as I see Mordecai, the Jew, sitting at the king's gate." Let Haman tell us, for he has had experience; let Haman tell us, for in the confidence of his friends he speaks the truth; let Haman tell us the true value of those glittering, those attractive things for which men so earnestly toil, through all their busy lives. Wealth, honour, earthly pleasure never made a man either wise, or good, or happy. It is not in their power to subdue the strength of evil passions; they are the very food they live upon. As wisely might we try to quench a fire with oil, as to allay the thirstings of pride and ambition and revenge by larger measures of worldly prosperity. What the Scriptures say of one such passion is applicable to others, "He that loveth silver shall not be satisfied with silver, nor he that loveth abundance with increase." Ecc. v. 10. Indeed no man under the sway of an evil passion is the keeper of his own spirit. The sight of one, who has never harmed him, may make him a prey to corroding thoughts; the silent rebuke of good men upon his evil becomes a torment; and, like Mordecai before Haman, he sees those as he passes along the streets, who fill him with bitterness.

How different is it with him, who in the language of a great worldly poet,

> "Feels within him
> A peace above all earthly dignities,
> A still and quiet conscience!"

See this exemplified in Mordecai. He is not honoured of the world; he holds an humble office in the king's gate; he is the special object of that stern decree, which has called forth his people's sorrow; but the calm of his heart, neither Haman nor Ahasuerus can disturb. If Haman is more honoured, Mordecai is more worthy of honour. If Haman is a prince, Mordecai deserves a nobler title; he is truly A MAN. What is the secret of the difference? The same that obtains in all ages and in every land. Not a difference of rank or title; of robes or wealth; of strength or learning. Not a difference solely of education. But deeper than all this, a difference in the sterling principles of truth, uprightness, and the fear of God, which form the character and control the life. True piety in any age is based on principles which exalt the man. True piety is true dignity; true piety alone gives true happiness, and lifts us above the agitations of the baser passions; while the joy of the wicked may turn to gall at any unexpected moment.

"Then went Haman forth that day joyful and glad of heart." But he teaches us that the wicked have need to tremble in the very hour of their highest mirth. His joy was founded upon false conceptions; and was felt upon the very verge of his destruction. He was elated that moment by the invitation to Esther's feast; but had he understood the matter, it would have filled his heart with terror. Thus is it with man; often fearing, where God designs his highest good; often rejoicing on the eve of sorrow. Indeed there is no reasonable ground for happiness for ignorant and sinful man, unless first he has been reconciled to God as his Father, has been purified as to his conscience by the precious blood of Jesus, and is going forward under the teachings of the Spirit of grace in the path of duty. He may be walking by faith as was Mordecai in that dark day; but he is inexpressibly happier than Haman. For he is assured that infinite justice, and wisdom, and power, control all current events; and he need not fear their unforeseen results. Infinite faithfulness is pledged that all things shall work together for good to them that love God. Rom. viii. 28. In short it is reasonable that the righteous man should fear nothing, whether prosperous or adverse; while the wicked man has just reason to fear at all times, and to fear everything. The pleasant garden in which he finds his delights is planted upon a thin crust over a raging volcano. His highest joys may prove the sources of his deepest griefs; and the hour of highest exaltation may precede but a moment his utter overthrow. "Then went Haman forth *that day*, joyful and with a glad heart. But that glad day, itself not without a drop of gall to spoil the sweetness of his cup, was the last day of Haman's earthly joy. The sun of the next morning rose to smile upon the exaltation of his hated foe, and to witness his own unwilling part in a stately ceremony for the honour of Mordecai; and ere that sun sunk again beyond the distant mountains of the west, it shone full on Haman's gallows. If men will rejoice while they are afar off from God, let them tremble also beneath his holy eye, and at the thought of his righteous hand. "Surely thou didst set them in slippery places, thou castedst them down into destruction; how are they brought into desolation as in a moment!" Psa. lxxiii. 18, 19.

We cannot but think that the conduct of Mordecai filled Haman with surprise, as well as with mortification, rage, and revenge. Men of an imperious temper are generally cringing and cowardly; so

Haman afterwards shows himself; and they do not understand the high sentiments of honour in noble men; much less can they appreciate the power of godly principles. Had Haman now been in Mordecai's place, the trembling spaniel would have fawned upon the hand upraised to take his blood; and have licked the very ground on which he trod, to supplicate in abject terror the pity of his foe. He cannot comprehend the courage that will not quail in view of the danger now threatening the Jews. He is mortified to find himself the weaker man of the two; and that Mordecai had a peace beyond his power to disturb. But Haman refrained himself. He is enraged enough at the immovable Jew to draw his sword and smite him dead upon the spot. But possibly the laws of Persia protected the life of Mordecai, so that even Haman could not touch him, till he had secured the king's approval. Haman restrained himself, not only from personal violence, but perhaps from giving any external notice of the fierce passions now raging in his breast. It is the common influence of much intercourse with the world, that men learn to school their feelings; and teach the cold countenance to hide the warm emotions of the heart.

We will not delay to notice long the consultation of Haman with his wife and intimate friends. He recounted all his grandeur and all his reasons to be happy; but how instructive, yet how humiliating, the confession that an humble Jew sitting in a far inferior place, could destroy all his enjoyment of these things! In the light of this scene, how poor are earth's best honours, riches, and pleasures! They are no criterion of worth. Earth's brightest crown may be upon the head of earth's greatest villain; earth's most splendid apparelling may fall in graceful folds around a polluted person; earth's mightiest intellect may be the world's greatest scourge; and the highest summit of wealth is no proof of the worth of him who stands upon it. The vilest of men may attain earth's most coveted gifts; and true excellence may dwell where penury and obscurity hide it from the notice of all.

The friends of the chafed Haman endeavoured to calm him; and advised that without delay he should claim revenge on Mordecai. This seems to show that the express permission of the king was needed, before he could reach the Jew; but they doubtless thought, that after what had passed, the king would easily grant so insignificant a favour. Haman proceeds as if the slight request was already granted; as he had done before in securing his lucky day for Jewish destruction. Indeed he and his friends had reason to believe, since a decree had gone forth for the slaughter of all the Jews, that Ahasuerus would think little of anticipating the day for the death of one specially obnoxious. So Haman yielded to the suggestion of his friends, and erected a lofty gallows that Mordecai might be hanged upon it. The shallow peace of a wicked mind was restored. The thing pleased Haman. Little dreamed he whose form should be there suspended. Little cared he for his rebellion against the people and the God of Jacob. "The wicked watcheth the righteous and seeketh to slay him; the Lord will not leave him in his hand." "The wicked plotteth against the righteous, and gnasheth upon him with his teeth; the Lord shall laugh at him; for he seeth that HIS DAY IS COMING." Psa. xxxvii. 12, 13, 32, 33.

But we may leave Haman and his counsellors anticipating a gratified revenge; and under cover of the shades of evening that have fallen upon the earth, let us turn our feet to the gates of the palace. Here is another of those instructive lines, which occur so frequently in this eventful narrative: "On that night the king could not sleep." We are not told the immediate and natural cause of the monarch's sleeplessness. If the record ran, "On that night Haman could not sleep;" we could easily conjecture a sufficient reason in the agitation of unhappy passions. Yet Haman possibly slept well; as does many a sinner on the last night of his mortal life. But on that night the king could not sleep. He complains of no pain or sickness to make him wakeful; he seems not specially occupied with business, nor specially agitated by strong passions, which banish his rest. It is one of those unaccountable seasons of restlessness, when we vainly court repose; and when the softest couch cannot secure it. It is no more in the power of the highest monarch than of his meanest subjects, to secure this great blessing. But though we do not know the specific natural cause for the loss of sleep in Ahasuerus, there was a good reason for it. This is one of those occasions which the most sceptical cannot explain without the admission, "This is the finger of God." There is a King, mightier than Ahasuerus, who never sleeps. On his head are many crowns; his eyes are as a flame of fire; he walketh in the midst of the golden lamps which he has placed to enlighten the earth. Rev. i 13. He knows not only the works, and the faith, and the patience of his people; but the opportune time to bring these forth to light; he knows the designs of their enemies, and the nice occasion when their well laid schemes may best be thwarted. The King of Zion is sleepless; and he lays a wakeful pillow beneath the head of Persia's monarch. If the king had not lain sleepless that night, what then perhaps? Would Mordecai have suffered death upon the gallows before the hour of Esther's intercession? When we introduce into the chain of providence, which Divine skill has wrought, a single *if*, or a single *perhaps*, we make room for a thousand. If Mordecai had already received some trifling reward for saving the king's life; if Esther had hastened this by impatience for her protector's advantage; if the sleepless king had sought amusement in music, or elsewhere than in the chronicles of the kingdom; a thousand ifs might have defeated the result. But

Providence made the king that night sleepless and serious; and he commanded that the book of the records of the kingdom should be read before him in those wakeful hours.

The Persian kings, as we are informed by the ancient historians, kept a kind of diary of events, in which remarkable occurrences were recorded, and the names of persons who deserved rewards or preferment for valuable services. The Jews do not fail at this point to introduce some fabulous and marvellous stories, to heighten the effect of this occasion beyond the simple dignity of the inspired narrative. The Former Targum says that the reader chosen by the king at this time was one of the sons of Haman; and the Latter Targum says that he opened miraculously at the very place; and when he saw recorded there the hated name of Mordecai, he turned over to another part of the records; but the refractory leaves flew back, and he was forced to read the necessary passage. This is man's method of rendering more miraculous the dealings of God's providence, which are more truly wonderful without the unlikely miracle. To us, it seems likely, that several hours of the night were consumed in restless tossings before the king gave over the attempt to secure repose; and several more in reading to the sleepless monarch; so that the night was far spent, and even day had dawned when the reader reached the pages which told of Mordecai's unrequited faithfulness. For when the king heard of this, and projected a reward for Mordecai, Haman was already waiting in the court of the palace. The entire circumstances following prove that day had now dawned after the sleepless night. This passage reminded the king how near he had been to death; and his conscience reproached him for ingratitude to his deliverer.

It seems obvious, from the manner in which the name of Mordecai is mentioned here, and the effect produced by it upon the king, that he felt no prejudice nor hostility against the Jews. It begins now to appear that, however guilty the king's thoughtlessness in signing the decree, he had no malice against that people; and but little comprehended the proclamation that had sent lamentation and distress throughout his wide empire.

Let us not be surprised if good deeds often pass unnoticed, and work no apparent advantage to those that do them. Should this be our experience, we may possess our souls in patience. Well doing is so much its own reward, that we can afford to have our most laborious and self-denying duties unnoticed by the eye of man. Let it be a comfort to know that our names and deeds are recorded in the chronicles of an eternal kingdom; that they are not forgotten by our gracious King; that if, for the present, they are passed by, it is not in thoughtlessness of them, but for reasons of infinite wisdom and righteousness; and that in due time the smallest service done for His glory shall meet a full reward. The books shall be opened and publicly read; and every secret thing shall be revealed. This is indeed no source of comfort to a sinful mind; nor does it lack its aspect of solemn awe to the most upright; "for there is not a just man upon earth, that doeth good and sinneth not." Eccl. vii. 20. If judgment for any of us, in that great day, must be settled simply by what we have been and what we have done, we may well fear for the opening of the books, in the presence of the eternal King. "If thou, Lord, shouldest mark iniquity, O Lord, who could stand?" Psa. cxxx. 3. Happily for us there is a way pointed out for pardon of past iniquity and for reconciliation to God; as well as a way of duty and righteousness in his holy service. When the books are opened, another book shall be opened, which is the book of life of the Lamb slain; and they whose names are there recorded shall receive the blessings purchased by his priceless blood. Our hopes of this infinite honour must be tested by the sincerity of our attachment to Christ, and the zeal of our obedience to his commands. Let us strengthen our love; let us quicken our obedience; let us renew our faith; let us keep in chief remembrance, that our services are rendered to Him who tries our hearts. Little matter if men know not the devotion of our service; little matter if the left hand knoweth not what the right hand doeth; little matter if our best deeds are unrequited on earth, or if men give us returns of base ingratitude. "In due season we shall reap if we faint not." Gal. vi. 9.

The sacred volume brings before us, most remarkably, the true excellence of human life; and urges us to secure it. In one of its narratives it brings before us a friendless boy, sold into bondage by the treachery of his own brethren, cast into prison by a woman's wickedness, and left to languish there by a courtier's ingratitude; yet without the guidance of a wise and loving father, without friends or wealth, or fame, or even liberty, it shows us Joseph, the wise, the good; despite of all his troubles, the happy; the benefactor of Egypt, and the Saviour of Israel.

In another narrative it sets before us a prisoner in chains, and under examination before the noble and the honoured of his age; and extorts from the lips of the highest dignitary, the candid confession, Almost am I ready to change places with thee. And the prisoner is not surprised. He would rather be Paul with chains upon his hands, and the peace of God in his heart, than Agrippa the slave of unholy passions, though he wears a crown upon his brow. The Bible has lessons of wisdom far other than the men of this world. Men say, Keep up appearances. The Bible says, "Keep thy heart with all diligence." Prov. iv. 23. Men say, Cleanse the outside of the cup and platter. The Bible says, Cleanse first that which is within. Men would teach us to bow down respectfully at the feet of Haman, the

Magnificent. The Bible bids us admire and imitate the upright, the conscientious, the courageous, the believing Mordecai. The true excellency of man must be found in his principles.

Please notice, that the Bible declares to us the true dignity of man; and sets before us the sterling excellencies for which every man may strive. "Seekest thou great things for thyself," Jer. xlv. 5—riches, or honour, or fame? How small is the encouragement to seek these in the real gain they bring, or in the prospect of successfully attaining them! But few among the sons of men can reach any high place of honour or riches. With all your toiling to reach honour, you may fail to secure it; just as you seem to lay your hand upon it, some more favoured candidate for a shallow popularity may carry off the prize. With all your striving for wealth, riches may take wings and fly away, just as you feel secure. To say nothing then of the unsatisfying nature of these things; nothing of their transient gratification; nothing of the feeble hold you have upon them; suffice it to say, not every man gets rich, who toils for riches; not every man gains honour, who aspires to it. But he that knocketh at the gate of heavenly wisdom, shall find the entrance wide thrown open; he that seeketh, findeth. "Blessed are they that do hunger and thirst after righteousness for they shall be filled." Matt. v. 6. "Whosoever shall call upon the name of the Lord shall be saved." Rom. x. 13.

Possibly you cannot reach riches; holiness you may reach. The pleasures of the world always have disappointed those that possess them most fully. The pleasures of piety are only the more satisfactory the longer they are enjoyed; and he, who has the most of them, is the most desirous of following on to know the Lord. The Bible holds forth the richest treasures alike to the lofty and the lowly. The pearl of great price is offered to those that will sell all they have and buy it. Matt. xiii. 45, 46.

And do not these scenes in the career of Haman bring fairly before us the thought, that the crisis of a man's life comes often at an unexpected time? The joys and honours of Haman have reached their highest point, at the very moment when he is about to fall from them for ever. The soul unreconciled to God is never one moment secure. The voice of wisdom says, "Seek ye first the kingdom of God and his righteousness." Matt. vi. 33. Should the crisis of life come unexpectedly upon you, are you prepared for it? Should the great King ask this day, What shall be done to this man for the past of his life? would he add, Bring forth the best robe and put it on him? He only is wise who has made God his friend, through a Saviour's blood; and is thus prepared either for longer life in usefulness, or for a sudden and an unexpected death.

LECTURE VIII.

THE EXALTATION OF MORDECAI.

A DAY of the most important business dawned upon the Persian court after that sleepless night; and the king is no sooner ready to enter upon the engagements of the day, than Haman is ready to wait upon him. What a faithful servant the Agagite seems to be! He is already in attendance upon the king at so early an hour; as if both he and his master had passed a restless night; as if eager for new service for Persia. When the king asked who was in the court, Haman was already in attendance. But we may not judge from the outward appearance. It is no affection for his master, nor zeal for the honour of the kingdom, that has drawn the prime minister so early to the palace. He has designs of his own to secure; revenge, that fierce and almost uncontrolable passion of a wicked mind, impels him; and the eagerness of his pursuit makes him blind to everything, but the gratification of his own passions. And to his excited eye, everything promises favourably. There is even no long delay before he is called to go before the king; and the way seems open immediately to make his request before him for the death of Mordecai. But the remarkable change which has taken place in the king's mind during that sleepless night—so different from Haman's object and desires—bids us note the finger of God in ordering the minutest details of our mortal life. The slow-moving interference of Esther seems about to sacrifice Mordecai to her negligence or delay; but even this is designed in infinite wisdom to secure more illustriously the relief of the chosen people, and to exhibit more gloriously the workings of their covenant God. Had Haman preferred his request the night before; or had he secured an audience a little earlier, before the reader of the Chronicles had reached the name of Mordecai, he might perhaps have secured his purpose. But Haman knows nothing of the events that have transpired, since he last saw the king; his ready invitation to come in, he interprets wholly in his favour; and he cannot suppose that at so early an hour of the day, any other serious business already occupies the king's mind.

Haman awaits the words of Ahasuerus as a servant waits upon his master. It is not becoming in the court of such a prince, that the subject should speak before he is asked his business, and permission is given him to address his sovereign. So when Esther came in, the first words were uttered by her husband. So Haman waits, expecting to hear from the lips of Ahasuerus, What wilt thou, Haman?

And what is thy request? The man, who but the day before had supped with the king and queen; and who to-day has a second invitation to a similar honour, expects a liberality befitting the state of the king. And if but the evening before, when Esther came in unbidden, the monarch had pledged that her request should be granted even to the half of the kingdom; if now the king seems to be in a liberal mood; surely Haman, when called by the king to come, may freely make the small request he came to offer. But instead of making the inquiry, What wilt thou, Haman? the king seems to open the door for larger honours to him. How gratefully sounded the inquiry of the king, What shall be done to the man whom the king delighteth to honour? Haman refrained himself from the promptings of revenge; for pride and vanity are stronger passions with him than even his hatred of Mordecai. How natural the thought of that heart, so wrapped in self and so elated with the advantages already enjoyed! Whom can this mean, but me? "Now, Haman thought in his heart, To whom would the king delight to do honour more than to myself?" How deceitful is pride! How unhappy is that world which is full of it! How wretched do we make ourselves and each other, when self and self-aggrandizement engross our thoughts!

Haman's past success and his inordinate vanity prompt the belief that these contemplated honours are to fall upon him; and yet as the king has named no one, he has the opportunity of telling his whole heart upon the subject with the air of a disinterested person. It might indeed have been dangerous for this ambitious man to propose such honours, if they had been openly for himself; and when we know that his secret thought was for himself, we must judge that for the safety of the king and the peace and welfare of the kingdom, Haman was an exceedingly dangerous man in the Persian court. Every reader of ancient history knows how frequent are the revolutions in despotic empires; and how often the monarch, separated by his state and his luxuries, alike from the sympathies and the knowledge of his people, is suddenly murdered, and his throne usurped by some ambitious favourite, whom he had lifted to honour and power. So, as the Scriptures tell us, Hazael put to death the king of Syria and reigned in his stead. 2 Kings viii. 15. And Haman, here, gives us reason to suspect that he entertained secret thoughts of treasonable ambition. Under cover of suggesting honours to be paid to another, he reaches forth his hand to grasp a dignity, that was regarded as peculiarly royal. Perhaps because the man, who looked towards kingly honours, was especially dangerous in those eastern governments, the Persian law made it a capital offence for any subject to wear the king's robe. Haman perhaps would not have dared to mention such a thing to Ahasuerus but for two reasons. 1st, the king's question allowed him to do this, without seeming to desire this honour for himself; and 2d, the ancient historians give us two examples of persons in Persia who did wear the king's apparel and were left unharmed; and if the date we assign to this book is correct, these cases both occurred not very long before this time.* It is quite likely that one of these cases Haman had before his eyes, as it occurred through the orders of Xerxes, when he made this representation to Ahasuerus, "For the man whom the king delighteth to honour, let the royal apparel be brought which the king useth to wear, and the horse which the king rideth upon, and the crown royal which is set upon his head; and let this apparel and horse be delivered to one of the king's most noble princes, that they may array the man whom the king delighteth to honour, and bring him on horseback through the streets of the city, and proclaim before him, Thus shall it be done to the man whom the king delighteth to honour."

Here we seem to have in full Haman's idea of earthly magnificence. To wear the robes of royalty; to be the object of the people's admiration; to enjoy a triumph whether deserved or not; these are the most empty honours of earth; these are the gay bubbles that burst the soonest; the splendours these, that are most speedily forgotten. Here we may see the true character of Haman; and judge

* See the cases cited in Gill, *in loco*.

that he who wishes to ride the horse of Ahasuerus and to wear his robes, would not scruple if he dared to ascend the throne. The king has reason to guard against Haman's ambition; and if we see afterwards that Ahasuerus saved the Jews from the revenge of the Agagite, we may judge from these indications, that the intervention of Esther saved the realm of Persia from revolution; and the life of the king from the ambition of an unprincipled favourite who now covets the regal robes.

What an unexpected—what a blighting stroke to the crafty policy of the Amalekite, was the answer of the king! Just as Haman looked for the nomination of some high dignitary thus to do for his honour; just as he expects in his hour of exaltation that his errand to the palace will be one of easy accomplishment; just as the vision of Mordecai's death fills up his imagination of that triumphal day, the mortifying mandate issues from the royal lips: "Make haste, take the apparel and the horse as thou hast said, and do even so unto Mordecai the Jew that sitteth in the king's gate; let nothing fail of all that thou hast spoken." No more astounding command, no deeper mortification could be given to Haman. Mordecai, the Jew! the man he most hated; the man whose nation Ahasuerus himself had doomed; whose life Haman came there that hour to seek; for whom, already, he had prepared a degrading gibbet! Haman was so proud and selfish that he would have attended with grief and envy upon the triumphal honours of any other man; had he not interpreted the king's liberal designs in his own favour, he would not have ventured so high a bid; but that all this should be for Mordecai, and at his own suggestion, was grief and vexation indeed. Gladly would Haman have avoided the hated spectacle; gladly now, for once, would he allow the precedence to some other prince of the realm; since the stately ceremonial must occur, he would gladly be absent from it. But the king has appointed him to do what himself has devised; and Haman dare not refuse.

And now the streets of Shushan echo with the shouts of a glad multitude as a procession marches in triumphal splendour to honour a man, who has saved the life of the king. Haman himself has stripped off the sackcloth with which his malice had clothed the limbs of Mordecai; and, with a heavy heart, has arrayed him in the purple and white garments of Persian royalty. The king's favourite horse is brought forth, and the crown is placed—not upon Mordecai's head, this would be too presumptuous—but upon the head of the horse. For this was the custom of the realm on occasions of great ceremonial; and even among the Romans the horses were crowned when they drew triumphal chariots. And the proclamation, "Bow the knee to the man whom the king delighteth to honour," was made by a princely herald; and the voice was Haman's. And now as they passed in triumph through the city; and the Jews stood amazed to see their bitter foe thus sounding forth the honours of one of their brethren; and the giddy populace joined the throng and swelled the triumph; perhaps they passed by the newly erected gallows, in full view seventy-five feet high, rising above the surrounding buildings, meant to be a conspicuous sight, and now quite as easily seen as the man who built it could desire. What a contrast between that emblem of shame, and this spectacle of triumph! Whether it caught Mordecai's eye; whether he understood it; whether his heart swelled in gratitude to God for his deliverance, as a token of the coming deliverance of his people, we know not. It appears afterwards, on that memorable day, that its erection and the object of it, were no secrets to the attendants around the king. No one knew better than Haman why it lifted its head so high; no one felt more deeply than he, the contrast between what the king did for the Jew that day, and what he would have done.

Let us notice here, as a lesson of practical importance, that all this mortification of Haman arises solely from the state of his own heart; and that his trouble is the pure result of his own wickedness. Very plainly the king did not design to put any slight upon Haman by the triumph of Mordecai; nor had the princes or the people of Persia any reason to regard this as the beginning of Haman's disgrace. It was one of the king's most noble princes that was to make this proclamation on behalf of Mordecai; and had Haman any cause to complain that he was appointed to such an office? The honours of Haman had not been transferred to the Jew; and he had no reason to judge that the king had withdrawn his esteem. The favour of the king is still with Haman; and he is mortified only because he hates Mordecai. The evil passions of men are their worst tormentors; and no wretchedness in this life is greater, than when a man is the prey of his own turbulent emotions, acting without restraint. The sea is troubled now within Haman's breast, and casts up mire and dirt.

The characteristic difference between the two men is consistently carried out here, as elsewhere in the narrative. Mordecai is as humble and retiring as Haman is proud and aspiring. The honour so unexpectedly bestowed does not puff up Mordecai with vanity; he takes no part in the proceedings of the day, save as they are put upon him. Godly men may receive the world's honours, yet they do not set their hearts upon them; they are therefore less liable to be injured by their inflaming influence upon human pride or ambition; and they can better bear either to be neglected, as Mordecai so long was, or to be suddenly called forth from their obscurity, as was his case, without undue aspirations. In our own history we can see similar contrasts. No man less than George Washington would take a "step in advance to clutch an impending honour;"* no man deserved honours more; no man wore them more meekly. On the other hand no man more ambitious and scheming, no man a more miserable wretch in private life or a traitor in public, than one who had every quality of honourable descent, and of liberal education, and of polished manners, and of penetrating mind to make him the idol of the people; no man more unworthy than Aaron Burr. See the modesty of Mordecai. After the honours of such a day, he quietly resumes his seat at the king's gate. We can hardly think that he would be suffered to remain in an inferior post; we cannot suppose that in the deadly strife between himself and Haman, Mordecai regarded with indifference any indications of the king's favour to himself, for his people's sake. We judge that he would gratefully and piously trace the honour thus bestowed upon him, to the kind interference of an Almighty hand. But just because he here discerned the workings of Divine wisdom and Divine energy, his faith would trust to God's hand for further workings; he would not hasten by undue interference the hour of deliverance; and he passes before us with the calmness of true dignity. He does not tarry in the streets as long as possible, to drink in the applause of excited crowds; he does not hastily gather the Jews together to exult over Haman, and anticipate the hour of God's full deliv-

* Irving's Life of Washington. Vol. i. p. 452.

erance; he does not hurry to seek an interview with the king whose life he had saved, now that he finds him somewhat awake to gratitude; he does not take into his own hands the intercession he had before committed to the queen. Mordecai uses his honour with a moderation that seems more surprising, the more we reflect upon it. He calmly returns to his seat at the king's gate. "He that believeth shall not make haste." Isa. xxviii. 16. Mordecai has calmly committed his interests, and the far dearer interests of Israel to the guardianship of Israel's God. And here he teaches us a new lesson of faith; different from those he taught us before, but not inconsistent with them. He has taught us before, that faith in God is the efficient spring of zeal and duty. When there is anything for us to do, faith bids us do it. But here Mordecai reminds us that there are times when God's people, having done that which God's providence bids them do, are called upon to leave the rest in his hands, and calmly to abide his gracious and powerful working. When such a crisis arrives, it is as wrong to be impatient, as at other times it is wrong to be idle. Perhaps Mordecai recalled the momentous period of his people's eventful history, when their hosts at the Red Sea, though beset by imminent peril, were commanded to "stand still and see the salvation of God." Exod. xiv. 13. Action, Mordecai has already taken. He had urged Esther to use her influence; he had assembled his people and joined them in solemn fasting and prayer; and now, believing in God and reposing upon his covenant, he can afford to wait and learn the meaning of the change, which God had thus begun, in favour of Israel.

But while dark adversity and dawning prosperity find Mordecai firm in faith and joyful in his God, unhappy Haman has no such support in his hour of bitter mortification and deep disappointment. Without real virtue, without true dignity of mind, he is filled with renewed hatred and tormented with fiercer desires for revenge. He cannot but look now upon the darker aspects of the case. Had the king named any one but Mordecai, he might have borne it better; and have even congratulated himself, that if not chief in the triumph, its details had been of his suggestion; and to him had been entrusted the honour of conducting it, as one of the king's most noble princes. But as the honour fell upon Mordecai; as Haman drew the contrast between what the king had done that day for the Jew, and what *he* had designed to do for him; as he knew how fickle monarchs are, and how speedy is the fall of an eastern favourite when once his foot has slipped; and as he had not personal courage to face the least appearance of danger, Haman is filled with grief and anxiety. He stays not to listen to the murmurs in the streets; he wishes not to pass into that palace, where Mordecai, still unbending and irreverential, and now feared as well as hated, sits before him in the gate; he dares not venture now before the king to prefer the request that had carried him so early to that morning audience. Haman hastened home mourning, and having his head covered. This was no uncommon symbol among the orientals of grief, confusion, and shame. So Plutarch tells us, that when the earlier orations of Demosthenes were poorly received, he went home having his head covered and in great distress. We may imagine how great indeed was Haman's grief, that he could not avoid giving this public notice of his mortification, though the king gives as yet no token that he feels any displeasure at him. Yet we can easily interpret Haman's thoughts. The human conscience is a wonderful power! It oftentimes runs far in advance of all the intellect can discern; and anticipates those divine judgments, which it is conscious are so well deserved.

Haman hastened to his house and called together the same counsellors, whose advice had embittered the unexpected occurrences of the day. But they have no comfort for him now. There is a lesson which few sinful men are willing to learn, save by bitter experience, that sin flatters only till the wretched mind is hopelessly entangled; but when the tide turns, everything begins to bear against his comfort and his success. Men wisely plan their evil schemes; and eagerly prosecute them; and enjoy their early success in them; and the counsels of friends and the deceitful suggestions of Satan are embraced, with few thoughts of future failure. This is all flattery. Little do they think that they stupefy conscience, that Satan leads them captive; little do they consider that God's infinite wisdom counterplots their schemes; and that his justice and power are arrayed for their destruction. But when God ceases to forbear and begins his judgments, then their companions no longer can afford them comfort; and Satan cares no longer to maintain his successful deceits. A good man's comforts are the deepest when he needs them most; the wicked are forsaken in the hour of distress. The chief consolation of the wicked is forgetfulness; and there are times and there are troubles, when men cannot forget. Miserable comforters are the friends of the sinner in the day when God begins to let loose upon him his terrors. Haman may remind us of Judas, the betrayer. The chief priests who abetted his villany and paid him for it, refuse to share his remorse. "What is that to us? See thou to that!" Matt. xxvii. 4. The apparent friends who counsel a man to sin, stand off or croak, when the trouble comes. The counsellors of Haman portend from these new occurrences, only calamity and certain destruction to him. A man's tempters to sin often prove his tormentors; and an enemy of God and his church can find in the end neither refuge nor comfort.

Well worthy of serious pondering are the further words of these counsellors of Haman. "If Mordecai be of the seed of the Jews, before whom thou hast begun to fall, thou shalt not prevail against him, but shalt surely fall before him." We cannot regard these words as the utterance of a mere superstitious feeling. Perhaps these men, like Haman, were Amalekites, and spoke the oracular words of a long and bitter experience. Or, this may be the utterance of a deeper impression widely felt among the Gentiles, and established upon the surest foundation of truth, that the Jewish people were under the special protection of Almighty God. And truly, the world has reason to know that there is an Eye watching over Zion, that there is an Arm enlisted to secure her safety, of whose watchful vigilance and almighty power, the foes of Zion may well be afraid. From the days of Abraham's early wanderings when God told the nations, "Touch not mine anointed and do my prophets no harm;" 1 Chr. xvi. 20—22. Psa. cv. 12—15;—from the days when the great lawgiver lifted his rod before the king of Egypt, and scourged his land, and desolated his homes, and drowned his martial hosts in the Red Sea; down to the wonders which God had wrought in Babylon for the protection of Daniel and his friends, the seed of the Jews had ever been victorious over their foes. Even when Israel sinned, and their God was angry with his rebellious people, it was a perilous commission to execute the Divine chastisements upon them. Learn of Assyria, and learn of Babylon, (Isa. x. 12; Jer. l. 18,) and in later days, learn of imperial Rome, how a nation may scourge

God's people for their sins; and yet for their own pride or severity incur the anger of the Lord.

While this is eminently true of the church of God in all ages; true of the Jewish church before they rejected the Divine Messiah, and were cut off from the believing succession of the sons of Abraham; true of the Christian church since God, by preaching the gospel to the Gentiles, has fulfilled the great promise of the covenant made with Abraham, "In thee shall all families of the earth be blessed;" Gen. xii. 3; we believe it is also true of the scattered sons of Israel even in their present dispersion. That most remarkable people are scattered now in all the earth; they are suffering now the judgments, which God denounced upon them by the lips of Moses three thousand years ago; yet it is the faith of Christians that they are reserved for a destiny more remarkable than their past history; that they are to be restored to the believing succession; Rom. xi. 24; and that with the veil rent from their faces they shall yet recognize our Jesus as the Messiah; 2 Cor. iii. 16; and Him, whom according to one of their own prophets, Isa. liii. 2, they have esteemed as a root out of a dry ground, they shall look upon, according to the words of another of their prophets, the Jehovah whom they have pierced, and shall mourn. Zech. xii. 10. They have been maltreated above all people; and grossly by those that bear the Christian name. But all such things are in direct disregard of true Christian principles. The

New Testament teaches us the deepest regard for the Jews. Much as we have received from their hands, we look for more. Large as the early revivals of Christianity were, we look for larger through Jewish instrumentality. They are not utterly cast off. God has mercy in store for them. Beloved for the fathers' sake, they shall yet worship with us; and their restoration to the covenant of our God and theirs shall bless the Gentile world, like life from the dead. Rom. xi. 15. It is no vain superstition; it is a prophetic and a historical principle, which we may read in all ages of the past, there is a final triumph for the Jew. The wise men about Haman have well read the lesson in the records of the nations. The man that begins to fall before a Jew, cannot find support in mortal power.

The fatal words fall like a knell upon the ears of Haman, echoing the forebodings of his own conscience, and tolling the end of all his ambitious hopes. If Mordecai be of the seed of the Jews! Full well did Haman know that he was so. This fatal truth was the basis of his great scheme of revenge. And now busy memory flew rapidly back over the long records of his ancestry, to tell how true were these words, No success against the Jews. Ah! fatal and far reaching iniquity in the sons of Amalek! Fatal infatuation of wickedness in Haman, which made the Jewish descent of Mordecai the very cause of his deliberate and wider malice! Against this reasoning, he has no plea to urge. His iniquities begin to come upon him; and a guilty mind is proverbially a cowardly one. How easy a thing it is to fall! A single slip of the foot, and it is done. No matter how high the sinner's honours; how large his wealth; how boundless his ambition; how great his pleasures, he stands on slippery places; Psa. lxxiii. 18; and he should not think that his descent will be as gradual as his rise has been. That morning Haman rose with eager anticipations of gratifying his revenge on Mordecai. He forgot one thing; that the God of Israel had ever given the victory to his people; and forgetting this, the stupendous madness of his iniquity but brought upon himself the more stupendous destruction.

But the words of the friends of Haman, which tell their minds of Jehovah's faithfulness to his covenant, are of far wider application. It is still true, that no weapon formed against Zion shall prosper. Isa. liv. 17. Whether they received the truth from history or elsewhere, God's holy word teaches it to us; and the largest readings of human history will but confirm it. Who can count the forms of opposition that have arrayed themselves against the church of the living God? "Many a time have they afflicted me from my youth up, may Israel now say; many a time have they afflicted me from my youth up, yet they have not prevailed against me." Psa. cxxix. 1, 2. Without, the church has been assailed by persecution, with the dark dungeon, the sharp sword, and the flaming brand; by the learning and scorn of human philosophy; and by the ever changing and ever vigorous powers of infidelity from age to age; and within, she has been undermined and betrayed by heresy, and superstition, and false philosophy, and cold formality. But the oldest kingdom on the earth, the most widely extended, the most actively energetic, the most prosperous at this very hour, the most influential, the most intelligent, and the most largely charged with the good of the race, is the church of Jesus Christ. Persecutors —even successful ones—have perished, and given place to others to die as soon. Sceptical delusions never last very long, and could never spread far but for the depravity of men. False religions have become more and more corrupt, to show most plainly that they are not of God. But the church of Christ is larger now and more influential than ever it was. The doctrinal views of Christians are more nearly alike on the most important points than ever. The duty of the church is better recognized in her relation to the world; and much as we mourn that christians give not according to their ability, the standard of liberality is higher than ever before since the apostolic days. Zion stands firm. "God is in the midst of her; she shall not be moved." Psa. xlvi. 4. "Therefore will we not fear, though the earth be removed, and though the mountains be carried into the midst of the sea." Psa.

xlvi. 2. This is our confidence, that dark appearances in the history of the church are designed to try our faith. We will yet believe that "the Lord God in the midst of her is mighty." Zeph. iii. 17. His arm can protect, and his truth is pledged that it shall. His infinite wisdom discerns the opportune moment when his interference will most fully bless his people and confound their foes.

There is no ordinary guilt and peril in being identified with the foes of God and Zion. This thought we should weigh, because we all are the friends or the enemies of Jesus Christ. His own plain declaration is, "He that is not with me is against me." Matt. xii. 30. And doubtless many a man shrinks back from the acknowledgment that he is a foe to God and to his church. The only way to prove yourself a friend is to come forth promptly, decidedly, and earnestly to take your place with his people. He will recognize you upon no less terms, than that you adopt the principles, and exemplify the holy practice of his gospel. And indeed you are a foe, if you are not a friend. There are principles involved in what Christ claims, in what he is, and in what he has done, from which no man can innocently stand aloof. If you can hear preached such a gospel as this, without decidedly embracing it; if you can hear this Saviour made known, without warmly loving him; if you can read the teachings of this law, without yielding it your holy obedience; if you can receive these teachings of Christianity, without cheerfully and thankfully becoming a Christian, there must be within you a heart at enmity to God. If no obedient child can hear in carelessness a father's voice, can a creature listen in indifference to the Creator's voice? a dying sinner to the only Saviour? They that are not with Christ are against him. Unreconciled sinner, you are fighting now, not the good fight of faith, but the evil conflict of unbelief; you are fighting now against your soul, against the Redeemer, against the church of the living God. If you continue upon the wrong side in this most momentous warfare, you must meet destruction. Like Haman, who had a Jew to contend against, you cannot prevail. You fight madly against the very God of Zion. Stay now before it is too late for ever. "Agree with thine adversary quickly whilst thou art in the way with him." Matt. v. 25. God now makes overtures of mercy to sinful souls. "We are ambassadors for Christ." 2 Cor. v. 20. He exhibits to you the gracious terms of pardon and reconciliation. Let not the pleasures and deceitfulness of sin flatter you, till it is all too late for your salvation; till God calls no more and withdraws his Spirit; till Satan cares no longer to keep up the deceit and your tempters become your tormentors. Certainly you cannot prosper if you either openly oppose God, or neglect the great salvation he urges upon you. Until you flee to Jesus and enlist under his banner, you are in peril. Every day of your life may be the last of hope and happiness; you stand upon slippery ground, and but a little may cast you down. Your plans and prospects may be fair in the morning; and before evening irreversible judgments may fall upon you. These thoughts are serious, because applicable to every sinner unreconciled to God. Weigh them, for the life of the soul. The only place of safety is the church of Christ. Every soul that truly loves him, bears his name, keeps his commandments, and promotes his glory, shall be safe in all the trials of earth and safe for eternity. But to neglect him is a fatal error; to refuse his service is eternal death. Every sinful soul ought to regard it as his very highest privilege that he may know the name of Christ, hear his calls, believe his word, rely upon his promises, and find his salvation. The day of fire shall reveal it. 1 Cor. iv. 13. The great King will then command, "Those, MINE ENEMIES, that would not that I should reign over them, bring them hither and slay them before me." Luke xix. 27.

LECTURE IX.

THE FALL OF HAMAN.

Does it not seem manifestly true to every thoughtful mind, that nothing of all the works of God can afford us better evidence of his being and wisdom, and power, and justice, than the remarkable displays of his providence? This book of Esther, and the narrative it lays before us, seem wonderful beyond the frequent workings of God's hand, only because the truth is fairly brought before us; is comprehended in a brief history; and we see the actors, the designs, and the results, all at one glance of the eye. But a little careful and devout attention would enable us to see things as marvellous in other parts of the history of the church; and indeed we may see no insignificant marvels even in the meaner affairs of an individual believer. God is wonderful in working; and rich in resources. It is as easy to show his glory in small as in great matters; and he can afford to lavish his bounty in what we call minor affairs. The same beautiful colours that deck the heavens in the bright rainbow or the gorgeous sunset, he can afford to paint with unrivalled pencil upon the modest flower that hides its head in the meadow. We must not judge him by our weakness or our penury. The Creator fainteth not, neither is weary, by the multiplicity of affairs which show his creative power, or receive his providential care. We will not say that God is *as much* glorified by the meaner as by the great affairs of his kingdom; but we may say, that he is glorified *as truly* by minor as by greater things. You may stand before a large and magnificent mirror, and it will reflect back your image, one finished and perfect form. You may break that mirror into a thousand pieces, and each piece now will give back an image, not as splendid, but as perfect.* So you may look upon the universe of God as one complete and magnificent whole which only he could create, and which shows forth his wisdom, and power, and goodness; or you may take the minutest fragment of this universe—a grain of sand from the ocean, or a single leaf from the forest, or a tiny mite from the swarming multitudes of animated beings—and each of these minute fragments of a world requires the power of a God for its creation, and the care of a God for its preservation; and his wisdom is exhibited in adapting each particle composing the world to its own place in the world's economy. Or you may

---

* Charnock.

take the vast providential affairs of the universe; you may see the

> Planets, and suns, and adamantine spheres,
> Wheeling unshaken through the void immense.

You may consider the infinite wisdom and power that so nicely balances them all; that directs their motions with precision so unerring, that men can calculate the very moment of a distant eclipse years before its occurrence; and from considering these vast affairs you may turn to the minute and humbler things which some think beneath the notice of His eye, but which are as completely and fully cared for by this infinite God as if he had them only in his mind. For man places in the ground the seed of some tiny flower, and just as correctly as the astronomer can map out the path of the planets, can the gardener anticipate just when the flower, whose seed he has planted, will spring and bloom; just what unrivalled colourings will be painted upon its unfolding leaves, by light—the shadow of God; and to just what purposes that plant can be applied in the period of its maturity. Man has but to study in both cases the laws of God. God's finger is in the great and the small; because no wisdom, no power, no beneficence less than infinite could devise or could execute any part of these plans; and all the parts are so nicely adjusted to each other, and so dependent upon each other, that no mortal mind can say what portion of all God's works could be spared, without damage, or perhaps destruction to all the rest. In our thoughts upon creation and providence there is no stopping point between the wide extremes. On the one hand, let us deny that there is a God, and consider all these works and all these harmonies the effect of blind chance; or on the other hand, let us wisely and devoutly recognize that God's hand is as truly apparent and as truly needful in small as in great affairs; to uphold the worlds, or to watch a falling sparrow; to guide the destinies of his church, or to care for the weakest believer in Jesus.

But we arrest these reflections to proceed with our narrative.

Haman and his friends have but little time for consultation upon this important and threatening change in his affairs; and the next incident keeps up perhaps, for a little longer season, the deceitful hope for Haman that all is not yet lost. While the wise men are yet talking with him; and possibly before they had time to counsel him at all hazards to make his peace with Mordecai; the chamberlains of the palace came to lead him to that post of unusual honour, at the banquet of the queen. Some suppose that Haman, in his agitation, had forgotten his appointment; and must thus be reminded of it. But thus called before the queen, the pride of the favourite is again aroused; and perhaps he partially forgot his mortification; and with at least some degree of composure, he went to the palace.

The select company are met together at the banquet of wine; and each of the three—the guests Ahasuerus and Haman, and their entertainer Esther—is full of emotions that leave little room to think of the delicacies before them. We are informed that it was the Persian custom to serve the wine at the beginning of their entertainments; and thus there was, upon this occasion, no long delay for the great business of the hour. Though Haman came there with a heavy heart, we have no reason to think that he looked for any disgrace through the influence of Esther; or that he had at all identified the queen with the cause of the Jews. We see now the wisdom of Mordecai in forbidding the queen to make known her kindred; and up to this moment no thought of her people had entered the minds of her husband or her foe. But apart from any apprehensions arising from the queen, Haman has enough to destroy his enjoyment of a feast on such a day as that! If he tasted the wine that was placed before him, it was through respect to his royal entertainer, rather than from enjoyment of the cup itself; or it was to drown the remembrance of that bitter day in the oblivion of inebriation. "Give strong drink," says the wise man, "to him that is ready to perish, and wine to those that be of heavy hearts; let him drink and forget his poverty, and remember his misery no more." Prov. xxxi. 6, 7. If Haman drank that day it was not for joy; and the little company was none the brighter for his presence.

For far different reasons Esther cared but little for the luxuries of the banquet. Her heart too was burdened and heavy; not indeed with guilt or shame, but with a weight of responsibility that made her mindful only of the important errand entrusted to her. An important moment of her life, hardly inferior to her venturing in unbidden before the king, had now come; the great request for her people was now to be preferred; and Esther was painfully upon the watch for the favourable moment to address the king. But even Ahasuerus himself is there in great expectation. We are told by Rollin that upon the king's birth-day the Persian monarchs, by established custom, granted the queen whatever she asked; and he relates the most cruel act in the life of Xerxes as done at the queen's solicitation. We have no reason to judge that Esther's banquet was upon the king's birth-day. It seems rather a private entertainment than a public feast. But the king came there that day expecting something. The delicate address of Esther, while yet she had given him no intimation of her desire; the evident fact that some deep secret lay with her, had awakened the monarch's curiosity, and had prepared him to be liberal at her request.

Thus each heart at the banquet was fully occupied: Haman with guilt and fear; Esther with faith and hope; and Ahasuerus with curiosity and love. So the banquet of wine was rather a great state occasion than a feast.

The anxiety of the guests, which would naturally embarrass Esther as she watched for her favourable opportunity, yet resulted in her inexpressible relief. For Ahasuerus too is desirous to come to the main point of the present interview; and it was therefore not long that he delayed to ask for her petition. How encouraging to her burdened mind to hear now the renewed inquiry, "What is thy petition, queen Esther?" and better still the renewed assurance, "It shall be granted thee even to the half of the kingdom!" Esther paused—we are unwilling to think otherwise—to lift up her heart in adoring thankfulness to the God of Jacob, and in devout petition to Him in whose hand are the hearts of kings, before she could trust her trembling lips to utter the long-kept secret of her kindred, and her great request for her life and theirs.

Deep emotion is ever expressive, ever eloquent, and ever awakens deep feeling in others. Great must have been the astonishment of Ahasuerus at the trembling lips of his beloved queen; at the deep feeling which agitated her frame; and at the amazing words she utters in his ears. Here is no common matter. He had perhaps expected from one that was so closely shut up within the palace; who knew so little of the affairs of the empire; and whose world was the world of women around her; he had expected some gift for a favourite, or some enlargement of her revenue. But he found it was a matter of life and death; of *her* life too, though she was an inmate of his palace; of the life too of her people. Astonishment kept the king silent, while Esther told the whole. "For we are sold, I and my people, to be destroyed, to be slain, and to perish; but if we had been sold for bond-men and bond-women," I had kept silence, though even in that case no adequate compensation could have been made by the enemy for the damage done to the king and the kingdom. All this is a mystery to Ahasuerus. He sees in it some dark plot that is to penetrate into his very palace and tear away his queen even from his side. He seems to have forgotten utterly the scheme of Haman, to which he gave a thoughtless consent; and not knowing as yet the people of Esther, he has no aid to his memory for recalling the transaction. In his confidence in Haman, he had perhaps never inquired what use had been made of his seal. He is therefore now deeply agitated by the moving recital of his beautiful queen; deeply affected by her tears; in the hasty passion characteristic of him, he is vehemently angry, and is deeply resolved to revenge her wrongs. He hastily inquires, Who is he, and where is he, that durst presume in his heart to do so? Now we see why Esther has planned that the adversary of the Jews should be present upon this occasion. His astonishment equals that of the king; for it had never crossed his thoughts that the queen of Persia was one of the victims of his malice. Policy, if not right, might have stayed his arm, had he sooner known this important truth. Every man that dares to do a wicked deed should know everything, before he can assure his mind of safety. The truth now opens before Haman, like a flash of lightning, which reveals a precipice to the benighted traveller just too late to stay the destructive plunge. The trembling Agagite has no time for long reflection. At the king's question, Esther delivers this prompt reply, "The adversary and enemy is THIS WICKED HAMAN!" The secret is told. The amazed monarch looks upon his favourite and reads the truth of the charge in his guilty face. "Then was Haman afraid before the king and queen." Guilt has no dignity; an awakened conscience unnerves the courage of even brave men; and a woman's voice, when it speaks the truth, fills the convicted adversary with confusion. Ahasuerus saw at a glance that his confidence had been misplaced and had been shamefully abused; and his anger rises like an impetuous torrent. In the excess of his rage he rushed forth into the palace garden, and every new thought strengthened the charge of Esther, and confirmed the proof of Haman's treacherous disposition. How strange it is that after we have long reposed our confidence in a deceitful person, have looked favourably upon his words and actions, and have interpreted everything in the best light, if suddenly we are undeceived and get one just glance at his real character, we are able in a moment to strengthen this just view by a thousand things unconsidered before, and we change instantly our judgment of him and of all we have known him to do! The change seems like the opening of our eyes, as if really we had been blind to all around us.

Whatever may have been the thoughts of the king respecting Haman, they were not favourable to him; the audacity of aiming at the queen's life and of abusing his confidence to make him a partner in the plot, inflamed his wrath the more he thought upon it; and when he returned to the place of banqueting, the occurrences there only served yet more to arouse him. Haman upon other occasions had seen the king's wrath; had perhaps awakened it towards other objects; and he easily interprets it now. "He saw that there was evil determined against him by the king." And now, at last, not with the spirit of a penitent, but as a criminal overtaken by the tardy stroke of justice, he begins to implore mercy. He arose and approached the queen's couch. The oriental manner of sitting at meat is wholly different from ours. They reclined upon couches upon a level with the table on which the food was placed. So Haman fell upon the bed where Esther was. There is no reason to believe that there was any other bed than the usual couch at the table of the queen; and it is in the highest degree unlikely that Haman had any such design as that imputed to him in the anger of the king. In an agony of fear he approached the queen; perhaps, as is common in the east, he embraced her knees and plead for mercy. He felt himself completely in her power. He was desirous of assuring her that he had no designs against her life; that he was ignorant of her kindred; that he was willing to employ all his influence to avert the decree, if she would only spare his life. But we know not the entreaties urged by Haman upon Esther; nor whether he had time, nor whether he had spirit enough to urge any entreaties. We know only that the attitude he assumed made matters worse in the eye of the jealous monarch, and hurried on his fall.

The first words of anger from the king's lips, are eagerly caught up by the surrounding attendants. Genuine friendship too seldom exists in despotic courts. If Haman had been an upright minister, the king's wrath would have found ready executioners. Envy and ambition are ruling passions in the high places of earthly honour; and where these dwell, there is but little room for an esteem that rests upon substantial merit. But a haughty and selfish minister, like Haman, would incur the hatred as well as the envy of the courtiers; and they would more readily join to triumph over his fall. The words of the king are quickly interpreted by the attendants. "They covered Haman's face." Among the Greeks and Romans they covered the faces of condemned malefactors; and if this be not the meaning here, it indicates, at least, that Haman is no longer fit to see the king's face. The favourite has fallen; and his end rapidly approaches. The gallows which he had erected for Mordecai, the Jew "who had spoken good for the king," is no secret in the palace. Perhaps the chamberlains who had summoned Haman to the banquet had seen it in the court of Haman's house; and the eager-witted courtiers are ready to do themselves a double advantage; by trampling upon the fallen favourite, and by bowing the knee to one whose star, they perceive, is in the ascendant. They knew, it may be, already the religion of Esther; and her intercourse with Mordecai was of course known to some of them. Taking all things together, and recalling the high honour that morning conferred upon Mordecai, they easily see the influence which must be produced, if the designs of Haman against the noble Jew are now made known. So Ahasuerus is informed of the gallows, presumptuously erected for the king's benefactor. This new evidence of his audacity is immediately fatal to Haman. The angry monarch gives the order that he should be hanged upon that gallows. Executions in the east are summary. But hanging was not the usual mode of capital punishment. Perhaps Haman was first beheaded and then his body ignominiously exposed upon the gallows. Thus sudden was his doom. In the morning proud and revengeful; at mid-day humbled and dejected; in the evening exposed in his wicked schemes, degraded from his dignity, and put to a shameful death.

But we stay here again in the narrative. And in resuming the thoughts already indulged touching

God's providence as here set before us, let us not forget to learn from his case that the lessons of Providence are not to be hastily read. What we are sometimes disposed to call the indications of Providence may the rather be the trials of our faith and patience. Providence seems often to teach the reverse of what it really effects. When the edict by royal authority was proclaimed in the Persian empire, God seemed to give the triumph to Israel's foes. The storms that sometimes threaten us, may only threaten. We have one settled principle by which to judge of Providence—God's Providence never conflicts with God's written word. There are apparent conflicts; and in the trial of our faith we may be like mourning Mordecai, or like trembling Esther. But let us keep firm our confidence in the word; and these threatenings of Providence will work us no harm. We are certain to be wrong if we so interpret Providence as to distrust God's word, or to murmur at his dealings, or to forsake his service, or to become hardened in sinfulness. When the workings of Providence, prosperous or afflictive, make us love God's truth more and rely more upon his covenant; when they make us feel that he alone can help, and drive us to fasting and prayer for Divine aid; when they make us humble and diligent and dependent, then is God honoured; then are our souls profited. These results, we have seen, were produced upon Esther and the Jews.

And may we not justly say, in the wonders of

God's providence—in the book before us; or in his later dealings with his people; or in the experience of our own lives—that we have proof of God's being, and power, and wisdom, and goodness, quite beyond the reach of any imposition? The wonders of God's providence deserve to be classed high among the evidences of revealed religion. The Bible is the only volume that claims for the Supreme Ruler such a minute and particular superintendence of his works, as will suit the facts we can trace in the history of man, or agree with our just reasonings in the case. Providence often seems a tangled web; and all around appears inextricable confusion. Many a Haman triumphs, and many a Mordecai fills the streets with his bitter lamentations. Many a cruel edict has gone forth against the people of God; and since God rules the world, it seems yet darker, that these have sometimes been carried into execution. But the end is not yet. Let the light of God's word explain his dark dealings in providence. And this is certainly true, that the darker Providence is, the more intricate its plans, the less we are able to see the end; and the longer it takes to effect its purposes, the stronger is the proof of Divine planning and Divine working when the end comes out right. In this book of Esther, how impossible that either of the prominent characters foresaw the end and laboured to bring it about! As we have said before, so many actors, and scenes, and motives; so many nice adjustments of times, and purposes, and events; so many dark threatenings of evil; so many unexpected dawnings of good, are things which no man can counterfeit. A history like this displays the finger of God as truly as the creation of a man or the control of the stars; indeed God's highest government is his control of free, moral, and even sinful agents, allowing them to display their characters, and yet doing his will. Such an exalted government we have shown in this book; such, God ever holds over the world.

We have good reason to believe that, if the pen of inspiration were commissioned to record God's dealings with his church and people in other ages, we would have many a record quite as wonderful as the book of Esther. We may call this entire narrative, a page torn out, almost at random, from the book of God's remembrance above; and transferred here for our instruction. God has the same covenant with all his people; the same principles of government; the same watchful care over them; he allows their foes to rage and partially to triumph; their fears to depress; and their faith to endure conflicts. The world has yet its Hamans and Mordecais; its present triumphs for the ungodly; its ultimate triumphs for the faithful. There is a practical application through all this book; and we should be more decided, and more prayerful, and more believing from the lessons we learn of Mordecai and Esther.

But the scene especially brought before us in the

present lecture, reminds us of the justice of God's providence in bringing retribution upon the guilty.

The long delay that often elapses between a man's sins and his punishment for them, has in all ages been thought a mystery of Providence. Apparent impunity in evil often strengthens the hands of wicked men, and they are encouraged to go on in iniquity; but the real design of this impunity is to exhibit God's wisdom, and forbearance, and justice, in the government of rational and moral beings. When we carefully observe the issues of crime, we learn that "the way of transgressors is hard." The entire difficulty and its solution are most remarkably summed up in the words of Solomon. (See Eccles. viii. 11—13.) "Because sentence against an evil work is not executed speedily, therefore the heart of the sons of men is fully set in them to do evil. Though a sinner do evil an hundred times and his days be prolonged, . . it shall not be well with the wicked." In the ancient Mythology punishment was represented as lame, intimating how slowly it pursued its objects, but it was remarked that it rarely failed to overtake its victim. So in the current proverb of common life, "Murder will out," we have expressed the general mind of man in the confident expectation that God's justice will discover and punish sin. But the wisdom of Providence is seen not only in the punishment of sin, but in the nature also of the punishment. Men often find their punishment springing forth from their own transgressions and partaking of their very nature. So the inspired writers say, "His own iniquities shall take the wicked himself, and he shall be holden by the cords of his sins." "He made a pit and digged it, and is fallen into the ditch that he made." "In the net which he hid is his own foot taken; the Lord is known by the judgment which he executeth; the wicked is snared in the work of his own hands." We may find scriptural examples, and examples in the world all around, that the sins of men are the mirror which reflects the image of their punishment. If Haman erects a gallows for Mordecai, upon that same gallows shall he himself be hanged. The Lord does to him as he would do to another that is more righteous than he. The wicked is snared in the work of his own hands. He eats the fruit of that evil tree, which his own hands have planted.

Though sentence against an evil work is not executed speedily, retribution shall certainly be taken against the most secret transgressors of God's holy laws. The only exceptions are made by the proclamation of pardon through the gospel of Jesus Christ. Let every sinner beware of the flatteries and hopes of impunity which allure him on, only until he is hopelessly entangled and until his sin is ripe for vengeance. A man may see no reason why his sin should be discovered; or he may flatter himself with resolutions for a timely repentance. These wretched—these wicked hopes have deceived thousands, and yet thousands more will go on, to discover in their unhappy experience that God is just; and to eat the fruit of their own way and to be filled with their own devices.

As the scenes of this book pass before us, it is not a hard thing for us to decide where our sympathies lie, and to which party we wish success. We may indeed feel emotions of pity even at the fate of Haman, though we recognize the justice of it, and rejoice at the deliverance of the Jews. And we shrink back from companionship with Haman, not because he failed in his plot and perished ignominiously. It ought to be because we abhor the principles of a man who could so deliberately plot the indiscriminate massacre of a whole people; because we detest his wickedness. Yet let us not lose sight of the truth, that while men die and generations pass away, principles, both of good and evil, are permanent from age to age. The links which connect us with Mordecai and Esther are the links of a common humanity, and, we trust, a common faith, and a common salvation. Haman but represents the principles which actuate those that stand aloof from the church of God, or oppose the progress of the church. The church was precious then, and is equally precious now; if we sympathize with her struggles as recorded in ancient time, we should join now to aid her in her conflicts with an ungodly world; if we admire the wisdom and piety, the faith and resolution of Esther and Mordecai, we should endeavour now to follow the footsteps of their faith. Let us justly consider *that* a spurious sympathy for Zion which weeps over her past troubles and takes no interest in her present trials; and our acquaintance with her principles and duties will but condemn ourselves, unless we adopt her principles and exemplify them by our practice. These things that were written before-time, were written for our learning. Nor is it within our power to decide that the times in which we live are of less interest than those in which Mordecai and Esther lived; nor that the transactions of our age are less important; nor that less dangerous evils threaten us. Perhaps no generation of men can ever understand the value to the world of the current events in their own age.

But one thing we may certainly know. Upon the principles involved in this sacred volume, one matter of infinite personal importance to each of us is to be settled in the times in which we live, and how soon for each one of us, it is impossible to know. It is to be decided whether your soul shall be saved or lost. And the day of honour to every friend of God may be as unexpected as Mordecai's advancement; and the day of shame to every unrepenting soul, as little anticipated as the day of Haman's fall. God gives sinful men warnings enough, without telling them when he will call them to judgment.

The principles of the church of God are the most ennobling that can be adopted by the mind of man; and only within her doors can safety be found for sinful souls. Those that have made a covenant with

God by sacrifice shall be gathered for safety in the great day of accounts. I may not forbear to remind you that some of you have never listened to the warnings God has given you. Divine vengeance against transgressors *seems* to sleep. But God in justice marks every rebel against his law, and every neglecter of the gospel. He will become weary of forbearance, when men are perverse in evil; and those who have enjoyed his most distinguishing favours may fear the earliest grieving of his grace. "Turn ye to the stronghold, ye prisoners of hope, even to-day." Zech. ix. 12. Haman stood up to make request for his life; but it was too late! The king's wrath was kindled. Have we no express warning of similar danger? "Kiss the Son lest he be angry and ye perish from the way, when his wrath is kindled but a little." Psa. ii. 12.

LECTURE X.

THE DECREE REVERSED.

THE work of Esther to secure the deliverance of her people is not yet fully accomplished; though she has secured the royal favour, and though the enemy of the Jews has perished. According to a common custom in eastern lands, the wealth of a state criminal is confiscated; and either is seized by the king, or transferred to some zealous subject as the reward of his loyal service. Doubtless such a rule instigated the cupidity of many to desire the fall of the rich, that they might secure the spoils; and so dangerous and unjust is the temptation, that the Constitution of the United States wisely forbids such punishments as shall affect the family of the criminal after his death. The lands, wealth, and honours of Haman, the riches which he had heaped up not knowing who should gather them—are passed over to Esther, and she placed her cousin Mordecai over the house of their foe. Judging from the amount Haman had previously offered to pay into the king's treasury, his wealth was very great; it had been his pride; he was willing to spend it freely for the destruction of his hereditary foes; but now the wise is taken in his own craftiness, and his enemies use his wealth against his house! We may trace in this the retributions of Providence.

Esther now takes occasion to make known to the king the relationship existing between her and Mordecai. Humanly speaking, she had run a great risk in concealing this so long; especially at a time when Haman was plotting with all his power for his destruction. Now that she informs the monarch of Mordecai, and doubtless recounts his excellencies with all the warm affection of a beloved daughter, her influence secures the high promotion of the worthy Jew. "The king took off his ring, which he had taken from Haman, and gave it to Mordecai."

This was the customary mark of exaltation to a place of dignity next to the monarch. So when Joseph was made governor over all the land of Egypt, and only in the throne was the king greater than he, we are told, "Pharaoh took off his ring from his hand, and put it upon Joseph's hand." We have no just reason to decide that upon the part of Ahasuerus this was a rash and unconsidered movement. Truly in the realm of Persia there were special reasons for entrusting so great power only to a tried and faithful man. Not only were the interests involved immense; but laws that claimed to be unalterable should be made with great caution and wisdom. And Ahasuerus has just had experience in his counsels of a reckless and dangerous minister, and should now be doubly careful. But Mordecai was a tried and faithful man. He had saved the king's life; the queen had long experience of his virtues; and the prudence and modesty and wisdom of his course are now recognized; and the monarch is justified in reposing this high confidence in this excellent man. What may a day bring forth! Yesterday the busy workmen erected a scaffold for Mordecai's execution; to-day the gallows has its victim; but the seed of the Jews has triumphed, and Mordecai is the prime minister of Persia.

But the work of Esther is not yet fully done. Haman is dead; Mordecai is honoured; her kindred is made known; and the Jews receive a new influence from the friends they have in the court. But so far as the Persian law is concerned, that people is yet doomed to destruction. The day is fixed; the decree has been published throughout the empire; and the changes that have taken place in the palace are not enough to secure the Jews. Their hereditary enemies, the Amalekites, are rather enraged the more, than subdued by the fate of Haman; the motives of cupidity and malice and revenge are too strong when they can be indulged under cover of a decree that cannot be repealed; and Esther fears, justly as the sequel shows, that the royal favour is too feeble a protection for her people. Some means must yet be used to make the victory complete, and to include the brethren in all the provinces within the great deliverance.

Even Esther and Mordecai are scarcely safe, since the law authorized their slaughter; but, supposing that no one would venture to attack them, their anxieties are enlisted in behalf of their nation. It seems right that the repeal of the decree, or measures amounting to that result, should be the first care of Mordecai, now entrusted with the king's seal; or at least that Esther and Mordecai should jointly petition Ahasuerus to that end. But as Esther has begun the work, let her carry it through. So she must again apply to the king. We are not told that her application was made on that same memorable day. It is enough to suppose, as we may, from the queen's deep interest in the matter, that no long delay supervened. Esther comes again unbidden before the king; but it is not so trying an approach as at first. Before, she knew not but that the king's apparent coldness for thirty days was proof of estrangement; but that her nation was known and herself proscribed; her coming then was an act of noble daring, but of trembling faith. Now there was the same peril, should the king refuse to hold forth the golden sceptre; but she is more hopeful of gaining her end. She is encouraged by her former experience, by a knowledge of her husband's love, by the favours he has already bestowed, and by her faith in Jehovah's covenant. Yet the approach is not without its fears. Esther does not regard it as a matter of course that she should secure her desire. She knows not that the king will do more than save herself and Mordecai. There is a difficulty in the way. He might wish to go further; but the laws of the realm are unalterable. How is Ahasuerus to repair the mischief of Haman? The queen therefore, in this second visit to the king's chamber of audience, shows more deep emotion than at first. She fell down at his feet and with tears besought him to put away the mischief from her people.

Let us consider this new position of queen Esther as of deep interest to us; as affording us new instruction in our duty. She now comes rather to plead for others than for herself; and her intercessions afford us a model of the interest and earnestness that should characterize our intercessory supplications at the throne of a greater and a more gracious King, whose name is blessed for ever! What judgment would we have formed of Esther in the palace, if in the first place she had thought herself safe, and made no efforts to overthrow the schemes of Haman; or if now she stayed her exertions because Haman was slain and Mordecai was honoured and she herself was beloved? What would we care for a faith that had merely the desperate energy to approach the king, when her own life was in danger, and which has now no deep anxieties—no ventures to make for her brethren yet in peril, since she regards her own safety as secured? Think seriously upon the question—what would you think of Esther's piety in such a case?—before you frame an answer to it. For it involves an important principle, which we all should ponder; and which applies, not only to the queen of Persia, but to every professing Christian. We must give up our esteem for Esther and regard her as a selfish and heartless being, if, because she is safe herself, she carelessly neglects the interests of her people, yet subject to that inflexible decree. It must shake our confidence in her faith, as founded in piety or prompted by God's Holy Spirit, or resting truly upon the covenant of Abraham, if we cannot discern that faith working by love towards her covenant brethren as well as towards her covenant God; if we cannot see that it purifies her heart from selfish passions. Say I these things as a man, or says not the unfailing word of God the same things also? "For," it is written, "he that loveth not his brother whom he hath seen, how can he love God whom he hath not seen?" 1 John iv. 20.

But if Esther may not make the king's palace her sanctuary, and the favour of the king her protection from the persecutor's sword, what judgment are we to form of that professing Christian, who has fled to the church of God as a safe asylum for his deathless soul; who takes up his abode there with thankful reflections, that the time of his deepest anxieties is past; and who yet has no new earnest errands to the throne of grace on behalf of brethren who are afar off from Christ, and who are exposed to the just sentence of God's violated law? There was a time in the history of this professed lover of Jesus, when his own sins were set in array before him; when he was in distress as he thought of the anger of an offended God; when he drew near to the throne of grace, and with many fears, and with deep earnestness, besought the pardon of his sins. Then perhaps he was willing to promise anything; willing to surrender everything for the feeblest ray of hope upon his troubled path. He came to the throne of grace to ask for pardon and salvation, like the first approach of the Persian queen who came with deep consideration and earnest fasting. The trembling sinner indulged the hope of pardon; his fears and anxieties for sin—perhaps gradually, perhaps suddenly—vanished; and because of new desires, and purposes, and affections, he was led to believe that his guilt was washed away in the blood of Calvary. Now he is safe. The storm is past; and the covenant rainbow smiles upon him. God is reconciled; his iniquities are no more remembered; his hopes are fixed on an eternal home. These hopes are precious; and better, and surer things than we have ever thought, are true for every penitent soul that has ever fled to Christ and received, through his atoning blood, the pardon of his sins. "There is therefore now no condemnation to them that are in Christ Jesus." Rom. viii. 1. The truly pious soul is perfectly safe for time and for eternity. "Who," says an inspired writer, "shall separate us from the love of Christ?" Rom. viii. 35. And his triumphant reply is, that there are no possible means by which Christ and his people can be separated.

His honour is engaged to save
The meanest of his sheep;
All that his heavenly Father gave,
His hands securely keep.

The Christian is safe. For him the hand-writing that was against us, is destroyed and taken away. The greatest question for any man is this, Have I truly been washed in the pardoning blood of the dying Redeemer? The most momentous inquiry of human life relates to a personal and saving interest in Jesus Christ; and no man should be contented with answering it once for all at any single period of life, even upon what appears to him the clearest and most unexceptionable testimony. It is a great fallacy to suppose that a repeated and intelligent inquiring into the grounds of his Christian hope is any evidence of his distrust of Divine teachings. A true hope of our renewal should be only the stronger for our frequent and serious inquiries into its foundations; and indeed such is the nature of a true hope, that he who never inquires thus may doubt if his is genuine. If any man is truly pious, his reasons for knowing it, should be better and plainer with every year of life; and the only satisfactory evidences are found in the workings of God's Spirit in the mind. We trace his workings by effects which he only can produce. The Spirit of God impresses upon the mind effects worthy of his holiness. "If any man have not the Spirit of Christ he is none of his."

It pertains especially to our present reflections to remark that if any man has taken refuge in the church of Christ, and is satisfied there with his own salvation secured; if the thought of personal safety relaxes his efforts to be holy and to do good to others; such an influence exerted upon him shows plainly that his "heart is not right in the sight of God," and that he has "neither part nor lot in the matter." Christ calls no man into his church to be content that the mountains of Divine protection rise around Jerusalem, and to be negligent of the very duties for which the church itself is established. If a man feels not for the wants of others, certainly the Spirit of God dwells not in his heart. An unfeeling heart for the salvation of others, never felt its own need truly, nor penitently mourned over its own sinfulness. Would we think it cold and heartless selfishness in Esther, had she been happy in the palace, neglectful of her own kindred, and careless of their continued exposure to that stern decree? Yet it is infinitely worse, if the Christian does not bow, with earnest supplications and with many tears, before the throne of God's mercy, mindful of perishing brethren around him. Here are causes for anxiety and solicitude far beyond the solicitude of Esther. If we have really the spirit of the Christian profession, let us look here upon the Persian queen and copy the interest she feels in rescuing her devoted brethren. How can I endure to see the evil that shall come unto my people? Or how can I endure to see the destruction of my kindred?—are questions of solemn import to us, and they should deeply burden every pious mind. A professing christian, not solicitous for the salvation of souls, well may doubt his own safety. Especially in the New Testament age of the church, and under the teachings of the Saviour's great commission, the best evidence of piety is a missionary spirit. The salvation of our kindred should call forth our earnest prayers; and the more we have of the spirit of the gospel, the more truly will we feel ourselves debtors to the Jew and the Greek, to the wise and the unwise.

But leaving these thoughts to your prayerful consideration, we return to the narrative. The pious queen is not satisfied with saving her own life and exalting her kinsman. She desires to use all the influence she has gained, to further her efforts for the rescue of her people. Her earnestness and tears are again rewarded by the stretching forth of the golden sceptre; and she pleads that the letters sent forth by Haman may be reversed. But the case is not without its difficulty. The folly of the Persian rule that forbade any law to be altered, placed a barrier in the way. It seems a very strange thing that weak and foolish man who must meet with so many clear proofs of his liability to error, through ignorance, misconception, and passion, should so much covet a reputation for infallible wisdom! It is most remarkable that the great Apostasy that sits in the temple of God claiming, among other Divine prerogatives, this of unchanging infallibility, should command the blind submission of so many souls. Does it not seem that the folly in the hearts of men to claim such infallibility, is equalled by the folly that admits the claim? But no evidence avails with many, to cure such vanity. "Though thou shouldest bray a fool in a mortar among wheat with a pestle, yet will not his foolishness depart from him." Though claiming infallibility, and having this claim allowed by the subjects of an empire wider and more populous than that of Persia, the apostate church has never been the same in faith and practice for any two ages—except as she has possessed the same spirit of pride, cruelty, and domination. It is only after the lapse of eighteen centuries that she has defined and declared as an article of faith a matter so important as the Immaculate Conception of the Virgin Mary; her highest prelates cannot foretell what new articles of faith she may yet add to her creed, nor of what mortal sin they may be guilty in denying what may yet rank among essential dogmas; and yet she claims unchangeableness and infallibility; and, her own changes to the contrary notwithstanding, her followers must believe her claim.

In the realm of Persia a long experience must have shown repeatedly the folly and impolicy of various decrees; and various occasions must have forced upon the government some expedient to correct the folly of that fundamental law that no decree could be repealed. So when Esther brought her request before Ahasuerus, and he was inclined to grant it, the case does not seem to have presented so great difficulty as might at first be apprehended. Experience had perhaps already suggested an expedient to evade the law; and yet the one here adopted, was so mischievous and so dangerous to the peace of the kingdom that it was wholly unsuitable to a case like this. It was here devised to set the kingdom at war with itself; to array tribe against tribe, interest against interest, and fierce passions against each other. The enemies of the Jews according to the law had full power to attack them; and this power could not legally be taken from them. It was therefore proposed to make it lawful for the Jews to resist, and even to spoil their assailants; and it was thought that their safety might be secured, if the influence and power of the government were thrown in their favour. It argues indeed very little for Persian wisdom and justice, and seems a very expensive way of maintaining Persian consistency. This we will more fully see hereafter. But it seems the only expedient that can save the

Jews; and yet preserve the rule of the kingdom. And perhaps Ahasuerus and his counsellors had but little idea of the fierce strife between Amalek and Israel; had but little thought that the struggle would be so severe as it afterwards proved; and thought the matter easily settled by a counter-decree. Mordecai knew more perhaps than he could persuade the king to believe; and his wisdom devised the effectual means for the safety of his people, which we will consider in a further lecture.

A new decree was issued by the king's command, and sent forth sealed with his seal, granting permission to the Jews to defend themselves, and to kill, and spoil their enemies, upon the same day appointed by the former decree for their extermination. Time yet remains to send the proclamation throughout the empire, for the important day is yet distant nine months; but there were also reasons for haste. To relieve the Jews from their anxiety; to prevent many from sacrificing or even from abandoning their property, and from hastening out of the empire; to prevent the increase and the insolence of their foes, it was well to publish the decree as soon as possible. To form some idea of the influence which such a decree might have had on the empire within that year, if no counter influence had been used, it may suffice to say that France, by the Revocation of the Edict of Nantes, lost half a million of the most industrious and thriving of her people; and this though every cruelty of imprisonment and death was used to stop the tide of emigration.

That was not a day of railroad speed or of telegraphic communications, but the riders went forth upon their swiftest beasts. Among these are mentioned young dromedaries. Such of these animals as are trained for running are very remarkable, not only for their speed, but for their endurance; and they are especially useful in passing over the immense sandy deserts which are found within the limits of the empire of Ahasuerus. Theirs was a different errand from that of Haman; and if revenge is swiftfooted, love is light of heart. The couriers of Mordecai went forth in joyful haste. Messengers of good tidings, they were everywhere received with joy. Shushan, perplexed before, is especially mentioned as joyful now. Perhaps Mordecai was well known there, and his promotion gave joy. But in every place the Jews were made glad; their friends waited upon them with cheerful congratulations; and they gave thanks to their covenant God for the great deliverance he had wrought for them.

In connection with this new proclamation, we have this interesting record, "Many of the people of the land became Jews because the fear of the Jews fell upon them." If we may regard this, as the brief record of a revival of religion in the ancient days of the church of God, it is well worthy of our regard. And we believe it is one of the scenes of religious interest which God has been wont to grant to Zion in all ages and in every land. There is indeed a very wide difference between the Old and the New Dispensations of the church in respect to efforts for the conversion of souls without. The Christian Dispensation of the church is essentially evangelistic and missionary; she is commanded to go forth and disciple the nations; the promised presence and blessing of the Lord can be looked for only as she is faithful to this great trust; and experience proves that the church prospers most, within and without, when she is most earnest in her aggressions. The Christian church is a missionary church; every Christian is a missionary; and should feel himself a debtor to the Jew and to the Greek. But the Jewish church had no such general commission. You search in vain from Moses to Malachi for a missionary prophet, except as they stood afar off to denounce the judgments of God upon the sins of the gentile nations, and as upon one occasion an unwilling Jonah was sent in person to declare God's word to Nineveh. Widely different was their dispensation from ours; and the influence of it upon the Jews was to make them bigoted and exclusive; careless of extending their privileges to other nations; and too often jealous that gentiles should come to partake of the blessings of their covenant. But though that was not a missionary age of the church, it was still by a perversion of Divine teachings that the Jews refused to feel for the darkness of the heathen. If not commissioned as we are to preach the gospel freely, yet their prophets plainly predicted that in coming days the earth should glorify the Lord, and all the kingdoms of the nations serve him; the native spirit of true piety in every age, would gladly welcome even the stranger who came to knock for Divine mercy at the door of the great temple of revealed truth; express directions were given in the law of Moses for the reception of proselytes; and perhaps there never was an age without its serious inquirers, groping their way from the gloom of the Egypt all around into the blessed light of Divine truth that shined upon the Goshen where Israel dwelt. Many a heart was made glad by such a welcome as an Israelitish noble gave to a timid daughter of Moab: "The Lord recompense thy work, and a full reward be given thee of the Lord God of Israel, under whose wings thou art come to trust." Ruth ii. 12.

We explain the peculiar nature of the Jewish church, by preferring to call it conservative rather than exclusive; and by referring to the entire Divine plan for the setting up of Christ's kingdom in all the world. It is a most remarkable truth—one which men have proved themselves too ready to overlook, yet one of which no intelligent Christian should ever lose sight—that the church of God was originally preached to all men; that twice at least, immediately after the fall and immediately after the deluge, it was universal; that the establishment of the Jewish church was avowedly a conservative expedient, Gal. iii. 19, which lasted only for one third of the history of man up to this date; and that even in its establishment a blessing for all nations was pledged. Gen. xii. 3. In the midst of general corruption, God separated a chosen people, to maintain his church and to perpetuate the doctrines of true piety; but the Jewish Commonwealth was to stand only until the "fulness of the time" had come; and when by a long experiment it was shown that the "world by wisdom knew not God," and when all things were ready for the coming of Christ, the blessing upon the gentiles, forfeited through their sin, was again to be restored through Abraham, and the gospel preached to all the world. Thus the original and the ultimate designs of the church were the same; and God's great plan of preaching the gospel to the world, seems ever to have been kept in view in providential arrangements. Especially by two remarkable means was salvation set before the nations even before the coming of Christ. *First*, the Holy Land, where God's chosen people dwelt, was so situated as to place the truth before the minds of the principal nations of the earth as then populated. Let any one notice the land of Palestine, and see how it stands, like a light house at the end of the Mediterranean Sea, surrounded by the great Empires of the old world, Carthage, Egypt, Assyria, Babylon, Persia, Greece, and Rome. The nations around could scarcely help but learn much of Jehovah's character and claims from this chosen central people. We believe that many important truths did go forth among the nations, and that many proselytes were made who forsook paganism to worship Jehovah. Especially we believe that the reigns of David and Solomon were blessed with revivals of religion which spread the influence of salvation among the gentiles, and the number of proselytes was very large that were incorporated with the Jewish people. Religion was purest and most flourishing then among the Jews themselves, and it had the most influence to attract the attention of the gentiles.

But the *second* means divinely used to proclaim the gospel to the world during the time of the old economy, was the wide dispersion of the Jews themselves. As the time for Messiah's coming drew near, the influences preparatory to his coming were more widely spread and decided. It is difficult to know how far abroad the Jews were scattered. Haman told the king that they were scattered through all the provinces of the Persian empire. But we know they were even more widely dispersed than this. More influence was exerted upon the world by the Jews of Alexandria in Egypt, than even by their brethren in Babylonia. They held a position of commanding influence, and they used the Greek language, into which they translated the Old Testament, and in which the New Testament was afterwards written. From the Acts of the Apostles we learn that many colonies of the Jews were scattered in Europe; while even Ethiopia on the South and China on the East received the dispersed exiles. Thus the principles of true religion were brought into contact with paganism almost all over the world before the coming of Christ; and while these scattered Jews prepared the way for the gospel, and became its preachers after the day of Pentecost, we can hardly doubt that much direct and immediate influence was exerted for the conversion and salvation of many heathen-born men. During the five hundred years preceding Christ's coming, many gentiles learned to know the God of Jacob, and to rejoice in his covenant; and this period may be called the dawning twilight before the rising of the Sun of Righteousness.

Many of the people of Persia became Jews. Thus even Haman's malice is overruled for good. God causes the wrath of man to praise him. So Paul cheerfully writes from prison that God was doing good by his bonds. In God's orderings for the church, prosperity and trouble have each a purpose to serve. If Zion was always prosperous, she would gather too many members of doubtful piety; if she was always enduring persecution, many of weak but genuine piety would be deterred from their duty, and her opportunities would be less favourable to influence others. The time of largest increase is a time of peace and rest. Acts ix. 31.

Many of the people of the land became Jews. Can we help but be reminded by this of our Lord's solemn warning, that many shall come from the east, and from the west, and from the north, and from the south, and shall sit down with Abraham, and Isaac, and Jacob, in the kingdom of God, but the children of the kingdom shall be cast out? If Persians became Jews, surely the Jews should have increased in piety. And we have a lesson to learn: if men born in paganism became Jews, is it not reasonable that those in our times who have been born in the bosom of the Christian church should become Christians? Yet it is to be feared that many of the heathen now press into the kingdom before those that have enjoyed the full privileges of instruction in the church. Many of the Persians perhaps were influenced by improper motives—through fear of the Jews it is said. Mordecai and Esther now possessed great influence. We do not like improper motives even for good things. But surely there are good motives enough that should press upon every sinful soul to bid him fly to Christ. The victory would be half gained, if men would refuse to be influenced by improper motives which keep them away from the service of God. And the motives to become a Christian, good and proper, are almost infinitely diversified. Men may truly seek for salvation who justly tremble in view of God's wrath against the guilty; and many are sweetly drawn by the attractions of Jesus and his dying love. It is unreasonable for men to object to any motives, while yet they refuse to be influenced by those that are the most opposite in nature and tendency.* And while any just motive may avail to lead an humble soul to repentance and life everlasting, how righteous is their doom who resist all the motives urged upon them by God's word, his providence, and his servants; and who with seared consciences and hardened hearts, rush to perdition in spite of mercy and judgment!

* Matt. xi. 16–19.

LECTURE XI.

THE DAY OF CONFLICT.

THE twelfth month, that is the month Adar, and the thirteenth day of the same, was a day of remarkable things in the realm of Persia, in the twelfth year of the reign of king Ahasuerus, Mordecai the Jew being his prime minister. That day was fixed by two edicts of royal authority, both equally in force, as a day of massacre and a day of resistance throughout the empire. The enemies of the Jews—so ran the unalterable law, might attack, kill, abuse, or plunder that widely scattered race; and on the contrary, the Jews, with the equal approval of a royal law, might not only offer resistance, but slay their assailants and take their spoil. It would have been better and wiser far, if the second decree had merely repealed the first; but the preposterous folly, we have before remarked upon, that allowed no alteration of a Persian statute, compels the king to set the kingdom at war with itself, and to sanction the greatest outrages under the name of law. It could not reasonably be expected, in any nation, in any age, or under the most favourable circumstances that the two decrees would neutralize each other; much less could it be anticipated, as matters then stood in Persia, that that eventful day would pass off quietly. Such is the iniquity of man, that if in any country upon the globe, a day was appointed upon which crimes might be committed with no other harm to the perpetrators than that which they received in attempting the crimes, thousands of bold and reckless men would start up, and that day would be marked by outrages of the most destructive character. The march of an invading army would be a trifle, in comparison with such a rising of neighbour against neighbour. Civilization would do little to mitigate its horrors, if indeed it did not aggravate them by teaching desperate men the more complete arts of spoliation. One such day as that in this fair land, would destroy more property, cost more lives, and bring more wretchedness, than long years of foreign war. The most thoughtful and intelligent man among us has perhaps but a faint conception of the large and constant protection we find in our persons, our property, and our families, from the ever present majesty of the civil law. And such a day as that would be worse than anarchy. Anarchy is to be without government and without law. The contradictory decrees legalized violence throughout the empire. Like the modern enactments for the destructive sale of spirituous liquors, it was the government formally legalizing schemes of mischief against the citizens whom the government should protect. That her own sons were to do the wrong, is no palliation of the wicked and suicidal offence. The edict of Haman was in reality a complete outlawry of the Jewish people for that one remarkable day; it legalized religious bigotry and every vile passion of the heart of man; and though perhaps the edict of Mordecai was the best remedy that could be found in the circumstances, yet unquestionably it enlarged the circle of lawless action, and put in jeopardy the lives and property of every family in the nation. If, on the one hand, among the adherents of Haman's party, there were daring and desperate men, who had malice or revenge to gratify, or whose cupidity was excited by the wealth of an industrious and thriving Jewish neighbour, they would seek by strength or cunning to effect their purposes. Or if, on the other hand, any persons, siding with Mordecai's party, really Jews or pretending to be such, had similar designs against any man or family in the whole realm of Persia, it would be no hard thing for him to feign that his enemies were the assailants; and upon such a lawless day as that, it might be impossible to bring the vilest wretches of either party to justice. When we look through the world and see that some of the most abandoned wretches bear the Christian name, not because they are truly pious, or exhibit anything of the spirit of Christ, but that they make a cloak of religion for wicked purposes, or that they have been born in lands where the gospel of Christ is preached, we need not wonder if many men devoid of principle were included in the multitudes of the Persian empire, who passed under the general name of Jews. And when we reflect that possibly many of the professed converts to the Jewish faith, became so only for the purpose of gratifying their own bad passions upon that eventful day, we may easily judge that the decree of Mordecai, though no doubt it saved much shedding of blood, did by no means allay the anxiety of the people at large. It filled the empire with fear. It awakened the most serious anticipations, not now in Jewish families alone, but in every household. For lawlessness can never be confined, like a quiet river, within prescribed boundaries ; but like a swelling flood, it spreads wide its scenes of ruin and devastation through all its course. No man could judge how far the passions of either party would carry them. The judicious measures adopted by Mordecai could do but little to allay the anxiety of the empire; and the people everywhere anticipated and prepared for, a strange day of civil war.

When the important day drew on, several matters greatly favoured the success of the Jews. Their first and most obvious advantage was, that they had the favour and power of the government exerted on their behalf. Doubtless the nine months intervening between Haman's fall and this eventful day,

Mordecai wisely employed in strengthening the Jewish interests; perhaps in displacing hostile officers throughout the empire and promoting his friends. So we are informed that the rulers and the lieutenants, and the officers helped the Jews. The guards of the royal garrisons were arrayed for their defence; and all who desired the royal favour or feared the power of the government, would refrain from attacking the friends of the queen.

But the wisdom of Mordecai secured also another important advantage to his people. By his advice the Jews did not remain each man in his own house and allow themselves to be beaten in detail; but they gathered together in numerous defensive bands. This arrangement involved perhaps the loss of some property, left unprotected; but it secured other advantages. It made them more formidable, and saved many Jewish lives. And doubtless it brought greater safety to the Persians, and freed the Jews from the responsibility rising from the lawless and irregular conduct of some that professed to be their friends. Mordecai could not prevent men from assuming the name of Jews; but these measures were wise to prevent the cause of religion from being dishonoured, by the wicked conduct of those who said they were Jews but were not. Those that were known to be Jews were organized in bands; officers were appointed over them; and their defence was a matter not of revenge or cupidity but of upright principle. These wise arrangements show the disposition in Mordecai to do all he could to counteract the evil plotted by Haman. For all the blood shed that day the wicked Agagite was responsible. What serious thoughts are these; that evil is so easy to work, so hard to stay; that a man's wickedness may bring forth evil fruits, not only months, but even ages after he is in his grave; and that salutary as repentance is, for the character and prospects of a repenting sinner, even repentance is unavailing to repair mischief already done, or to stay the evil influence of his misconduct upon others!

The Jews, being thus regularly organized for self-defence by the prudent sagacity of Mordecai, were also restrained far within the limits of the decree. We are expressly told that they did not lay hands upon the spoil. If the warfare had been conducted in an irregular and lawless manner, allowing every man to do that which was right in his own eyes; if, in other words, Mordecai had consented to use Haman's weapons—for his decree contemplated just such lawless warfare, and the counter decree allowed it to the Jews—then would it have been impossible to restrain many from enriching themselves, when their passions were thoroughly aroused; and thus unoffending citizens might have suffered. No such scenes of outrage were perpetrated by the Jewish party that day. Mordecai desires to secure the character of God's covenant people free from all reproaches; he would place them as far as possible above the suspicion of improper motives; he would use only such severity as self defence required; and therefore the command was given to lay no hand upon the spoil.

It seems strange that the Jews found any serious molestation upon that day after such preparations for defence. With the favour of the government, with bands well trained, and especially when the great leader of the opposition was dead, we might suppose they would be let alone. And certainly the blame, in the whole matter, rests upon their enemies. Not only did Haman, without just cause, begin the strife, but on that day—it is worthy of distinct notice—the Jews had power only to defend and not to attack. Acting solely upon the defensive, they had no responsibility for the slaughter committed; and our wonder is greater that their determined enemies should not retire from the now unequal conflict.

But we may suppose that during two months while Haman lived, and every body expected the decree to go into effect, many provocations had been thrown out against the Jews; and many avowed themselves to be their foes who were afterwards ashamed to draw back. When men begin an evil course, it is often very hard to get right; the longer they go on the worse; and there seem many reasons for going forward.

Among the reasons for bringing on so fierce a conflict upon that day we may suppose that envy and religious bigotry were the chief exciting causes. Doubtless many were envious of Mordecai's elevation. A Jew, and of an humble station, raised to so dignified a place, and using his power to sustain his own people, would necessarily arouse revenge and jealousy, especially in those that fell as he rose. But beside these political causes for strife, the Jews had many mortal foes in the realm of Persia. For the sake of explicitly bringing the matter before us, we may divide the enemies of the Jews into five classes, each distinct in itself, but altogether making a formidable opposition even to the kindred of the queen.

1. We class first, because already mentioned, disappointed political aspirants, envious of the Jews for their present favour from the throne.

2. There always has been opposition in this sinful world to the church of God; and wherever true piety exists, it will meet with hostility. The friendship of the world is enmity with God. This enmity began with man's apostasy; and with numberless changes of form in different ages and persons, it has been restless, and sleepless, and undying ever since. It is the vestal fire upon the altar in the temple of Satan, and never goes out. It burned in the heart of Cain when he slew his brother; and the single and sufficient reason in the Scriptures for the first fratricide is the contrast of their characters and deeds: "His own works were evil, and his brother's righteous." This hatred of the world against the church, exhibits itself all around us, in a thousand forms, both open and concealed; it arrayed

itself against the Jews on that day; and this alone sufficiently accounts for the madness with which they were attacked throughout the realm.

3. Allied to these enemies by religious bigotry, but having peculiar reasons for rage and spitefulness, we may rank the various pagan priesthoods of the kingdom. Many of the people of the land became Jews. This could not occur without arousing the hostility of the priests. The church of God has suffered much in all ages from the fanaticism and bigotry, the covetousness and ambition, of a wicked priesthood. Every intelligent reader of history, capable of discriminating between the healthful influence of true religion, and the destroying power of priestly domination, will understand that the priests of the wide empire would do much to promote this fanatical warfare.

4. The fourth class of enemies might consist of tribes that formerly lived near the land of Palestine, and were now captives and exiles like the Jews themselves. These had formerly had war with the Jews, and were willing to embrace the opportunity of renewing their hostility and gratifying their revenge.

5. The fifth class, allied to these but deserving special mention in this connection for obvious reasons, would be the Amalekites, the peculiar and hereditary foes of the Jews. Haman, we have seen, was the chief of these. We have no means of ascertaining their number; but it was no doubt great enough to form an important element in the strife.

It is most likely that the Amalekites, with the ten sons of Haman at their head, led on the desperate assault. Stung to madness by the remembrance of their ancient animosity, by the disgrace of Haman, by the loss of the royal favour, and by almost every motive that could kindle political rancour or religious bigotry, they were ready to risk all in the effort to avenge themselves.

When we consider these different classes of enemies to the Jews, it is not so surprising that the strife was not ended by the issuing of Mordecai's decree; and that the dawning of that day was anticipated with anxiety.

Time brought duly round the appointed period here emphatically called "the day that the enemies of the Jews hoped to have power over them." To the pagan party it was a "lucky day;" a day chosen by lot by Haman after an appeal to his gods to help him. That these vain gods could not deliver Haman himself, has not destroyed the confidence of his followers. They trust that they shall find the Jews too weak for them. The vigour of the attack may be understood from the simple record that 75,000 men perished on the side of the pagan party. This however would be but an average of six hundred men in each of the provinces of the empire. The aggregate was large; but it was a barbarous age, a fierce warfare, and upon a day set apart for lawlessness and animosity, for cupidity and revenge. The heaviest attack was probably made in Shushan and upon the very palace of Ahasuerus himself. In the royal city eight hundred men were slain of the pagan party; five hundred upon the first day at the palace, and three hundred the next day; and Ahasuerus had too good reason to see that Esther was not too much in earnest when she plead for the life of her people. Upon such a day, while other laws were laid aside, that one was also forgotten that sackcloth might not enter the king's gates. Grim visaged war, authorized by the monarch's own decree, dared to enter; and death revelled that day in the halls of Persian royalty. What a contrast between these scenes and those with which the book began, when the princes of Persia were gathered there for six months of feasting!

The palace would naturally be the chief point of attack, and there the most desperate fighting would occur. The Amalekites led on the war. The ten sons of Haman, burning with religious fanaticism, with mortification for their father's disgrace, and with revenge for his ignominious death, were at their head. The desperate nature of the battle there, is shown by the death of all these sons upon the spot. They attacked the palace chiefly, because there their enemies were, and they had full power by the law to slay Esther and Mordecai if they could. The decree was in full force that they might slay whatever Jews they could; and they would rather have slain these two, than half the rest of the Jewish nation. If even they slew the queen they did but what the law allowed. And if Ahasuerus should lose Esther, he could fill her place as easily as the place of Vashti. And we must acknowledge the superior policy of this plan. If there was any wisdom in carrying on the war at all, it was the strongest point of policy to make the main attack upon the palace itself. It would be a great victory, if, at the loss of many lives, they could strike down Mordecai; or if Haman's own sons could revenge on Esther herself, the fall and death of their father.

It was no false estimate that Mordecai had formed of Israel's foes; and no false alarm that he had sounded in Esther's ears, when he said to her, "Think not that thou shalt escape in the king's house more than all the Jews." Add to these thoughts that these very foes of Israel once possessed the honours of the palace; that they knew the avenues of access and the best methods of making an attack upon it; and that in all likelihood they had many secret friends still in power, and even perhaps holding places of trust about the queen herself; and we need not be surprised that a severe struggle took place at Shushan and in the palace.

At the close of that fatal day, the king addressed Esther and asked what was her further desire. It does not appear that she came again to ask any new thing. Ahasuerus himself has seen enough of the enmity of her foes, and voluntarily offers to grant further requests. And if in the first view of Esther's new request she seems to go too far, and perhaps to indulge in a vindictive spirit, let us fully understand the case before we form our judgment. It would be no great wonder indeed if in the fierce excitements of that day, and with the bloody bodies of five hundred foes and perhaps nearly as many friends in the very palace, Esther had found it no easy task to keep down the rising of unholy feelings; but we think justice and sound policy, apart from revenge, will warrant her further demands. She asks that the decree may be so extended as to justify the Jews in a second day's warfare; and that the bodies of Haman's sons might be exposed upon the gallows. So far as these sons of Haman are concerned, we may remark that they were Amalekites, and the curse of God was still upon them, and the Israelites could make no peace with them; that they had abundant opportunities to escape from Shushan within the past nine months, or even that day they might have remained safely at home; that they were the assailants and chief instigators of the war, and deserved to be treated as rebel ringleaders who had fallen that day with arms in their hands; that it was highly necessary to strike terror to the enemies of the Jews; and that the practice of exposing publicly the bodies of great criminals has been common in all ages. As before remarked, hanging was not the usual method of capital punishment; but the method of exposing the body after death. As to the war of another day, the Jews were still upon the defensive. It was necessary for their protection that they should be upon their guard; and that the officers and guards of the emperor should stand by them. The defeat of the first day but aroused the greater animosity of their foes; and had they found the Jews unprepared, they would have fought without the colour of law. By appointing this second day the Jews were kept from scattering; the king exhibited his determination to support them; and the advantage was given them in case any legal question should arise touching their defence. But the sufficient vindication of Esther and the Jews is the fact that they acted wholly upon the defensive; and the responsibility of the bloodshed was upon the assailants. It is likely the safe victory could not have been secured at less expense. The Jews as a matter of principle did less than the law allowed; did not lay their hands upon the spoil; and only slew those that, as the allies of paganism, tried to take their lives.

It seems a strange thing indeed; and yet the world has reason enough to understand how true it is, that a kingdom so holy and so beneficent as the church of the living God, cannot exist in this fallen world, without being the occasion of strifes and divisions among men. Even the Prince of Peace himself has said, "Think not that I am come to send peace upon earth; I am not come to send peace but a sword." The principles of the gospel are peaceful, and of course all its legitimate tendencies are so too; but to introduce these holy principles into a sinful world is often the stirring up of strifes, tumults, persecutions, and revolutions. It is a matter of interesting inquiry, How far is the gospel of Christ responsible for these results? And the proper reply is that Christ and his gospel are not at all responsible for these wicked things. Men professing religious principles have often been fanatical, persecuting, and injurious; but all this by departing from the principles of true religion. It is one of the necessary penalties of everything truly valuable, that it is liable to be counterfeited; and religion, the most valuable thing in the world, is no exception. Indeed it is the honour of religion, rather than the reverse, that it most of all things has been basely counterfeited; and man's duty, here and elsewhere, is to separate the precious from the vile; to receive only the true among many false. The true position of piety in all ages is that which the Jews here exhibit. God's people hold and proclaim the principles of truth and peace; but they use carnal weapons only in self defence, when they stand by their principles and use legitimate means to set them forth. The religion of the Bible may be defended by the sword; but it may not so be propagated. This is the example of the Jews in Persia. Their enemies had malice enough to attack them; and let their foes bear the responsibility. So in the days of early Christianity, the gospel stirred up strife; but the real cause was the malice of its assailants. Surely Christianity is not responsible for the strifes where she was simply the victim and not the assailant; where she meekly poured forth the blood of her children, not of her foes; and where, keeping inside of man's inalienable rights, she did not even exert herself in self defence. Making all due allowance for the occasional rashness and bigotry of good men in various ages; carefully distinguishing the madness and wickedness of persecution by professed friends of religion, whose spirit was far apart from the spirit of Jesus, we may justly say that all the troubles in the world, apparently originating from the church of God, have really arisen from the wickedness of men setting themselves in opposition to the holy principles of piety. We may well stand amazed at the madness and folly of man's sin! What insanity is it for immortal men to fight against the only hopes of eternal life, that are worthy of the name; against the holiest principles ever proclaimed; against their own true happiness; against God himself! It had been true honour and dignity had Haman and his party forsaken their dumb idols and bowed down before the unseen God of Mordecai. It had been true policy had the Roman emperors adopted, rather than persecuted, the holy and ennobling religion of Jesus. It had been true glory for apostate Rome to cherish and exalt the sacred Scriptures, rather than to burn and curse those who read them.

Are the sufferers to blame for the sins of their persecutors? Even when weapons of self defence have been used, are we to charge upon the defenders the sin of the assailants? The gospel is holy, if men are mad. Its teachings are a blessing to our race, and its hopes are light in a world of darkness, if even it does "turn the world upside down." It arouses evil passions, because wicked men wish no disturbance. It is thoroughly foreign to the spirit of ungodly men, because ungodly men are wrong. When truth may be reviled for differing from error; when light may be reproached for dispelling darkness; when good may be rejected for not agreeing with evil; when justice is despised, because it knows no fraud; when holiness is blamed, because it has no fellowship with sin; then let Christ be rejected, because he has no concord with Belial; and his gospel refused, because sinful men war against it; and his people reproached, because they suffer for righteousness' sake.

But if we wonder at the opposition of ungodly men in bygone days, against the church of God, is it not even a greater marvel to see the claims of piety yet resisted by men who have been born in the bosom of the Christian church, who have been trained in her principles, and who see their own danger and ruin in neglecting their duty? We can account for Haman's malice against the Jewish name; he was educated in all the hatred of a hereditary foe. But men born in Christian lands, having had Christian parents and a pious training, whose feet visit the sanctuary, and whose hearts have often pondered their duty to the Redeemer, yet remain enemies of the cross of Christ. Many indeed are not the avowed enemies of the gospel. But this only makes it a matter of greater wonder, why they can so long, and with so much indifference, stand in such a position, that the Scriptures themselves can charge them with hostility. If any man really loves Christ and his service, why does he not decidedly and earnestly avow that love? why not join in the ranks of Christ's people and serve Christ with an obedient heart? Why will men allow themselves to neglect the plain calls of duty for so many years; and never take a decided stand? The very fact that they can remain so, shows their true character. "He that is not with me is against me." When the understanding is convinced that this is the path of duty; when the conscience declares that they should love Jesus; it appears so much the worse that any can delay or refuse to side with the avowed friends of Jesus.

This day of fearful conflict in the Persian Empire is an emblem of the strife existing, every day, in every age, in all the earth, between the church and the world. The victory in this strife shall remain with the church of God. The battle is raging now, and the tide of success seems often to turn against Zion. The enemy often raises a shout of triumph. On that day many of the Jews fell by the hands of their foes. But the issue was for them. In the great battle all the friends of Christ shall be crowned with victory, and every foe shall perish. Sinful men contend, not simply against the church, but against the Head of the church; not alone against truth, but against the God of truth. The conflict is vain; the apparent success delusive. "Hast thou an arm like God?" And vain and delusive is every excuse. It is vain to say you are not fighting against him; vain to indulge in frivolous excuses. The only course of true wisdom and safety is to cast away every rebellious thought; to draw near to God; to receive the teachings of his word; to accept the offers of his salvation. You cannot too much admire the riches of that forgiving mercy which so long forbears with the sinful sons of men; and which continues to offer terms of pardon even to the rebellious. But forget not that thousands have presumed too far upon the Divine forbearance; and have delayed the period of their submission to the Almighty king until no terms of submission would be accepted. If the holy Scriptures lay great stress upon our accepting the just terms of the gospel, they insist with no less urgency that men should consider and embrace the right time of the Lord's mercy.

If the Jews were a terror to their foes in the day of their defence, who shall stand when God riseth up to judgment?

LECTURE XII.

THE FEAST PURIM.

The great day of conflict was now past. If we are right in supposing that, besides the sons of Haman, many of those slain in the battle were Amalekites, this is their last appearance upon the page of history; and with the last effort of the Agagite, closed a long struggle with the church of God. Here then was fulfilled a prophecy uttered many centuries before by the lips of Balaam, "And when he looked on Amalek, he took up his parable and said, Amalek was the first of the nations, but his latter end shall be that he perish for ever." Num. xxiv. 20. We have long previously remarked that the first battle fought by the children of Israel after leaving Egypt, was with Amalek, Exod. xvii. 8; and as the book of Esther closes the historical records of the old Testament, we may look back upon the warfare with deep interest. For Amalek is a scriptural type of our spiritual foes; and there is a lesson for us where our true strength lies. Amalek was no despicable foe; and had

Israel stood alone, the tide of victory might have been adverse. Look back to the first battle fought by Joshua, that great Israelitish leader; and while you recall the doubtful strife, gaze up to the neighbouring hill top, where Moses holds up his heavy hands to heaven, and where Aaron and Hur prevent the prevalence of Amalek. Look back to David, greatly distressed while he pursues Amalek, and read there also, "David encouraged himself in the Lord his God." 1 Sam. xxx. 6. Remember, too, that this last strife which ends with the sword of Mordecai, began with Esther's prayer and fasting. The strength of Zion against Zion's foes is not Zion's strong right arm; but the cry of her prophets, and her kings, and her feeble women in the ear of Zion's King.

After such a victory, it was becoming that the Jews should rejoice. The deliverance was great; it was effected by the evident blessing of their covenant God; and they rejoiced in it the more, as a triumph over that foe, whom God had commanded them to smite. And here we have a scriptural model, after which we might properly fashion our Thanksgiving days: "days of feasting and joy, and of sending portions one to another, and *gifts to the poor.*" And surely gifts to the poor are especially becoming, when the very object of the thanksgiving is God's providential bounty.

But the Jewish people were not content with rejoicing over their victory at that time. Haman's lucky day was set apart from that time even down to the present, as a day whose anniversary should be celebrated; showing thus their sense of the greatness of the victory, and their gratitude to Him who granted it. This feast is still observed by the scattered Jewish people. On the thirteenth day of the month Adar, which corresponds to February or March in our reckoning, they observe a fast in remembrance of the fast of Esther, when she went before the king. In the evening of the fourteenth, and on the morning of the fifteenth day of the month, there is a service in the synagogue; and they commemorate the happy deliverance recorded in the book of Esther. The Chazan, or Reader, reads and explains the entire book of Esther, which is written on vellum and rolled up like the Pentateuch; and this book has the honour of being written upon a separate roll, and is called Megillah or the volume. When the reader has opened the book, he pronounces three prayers, giving thanks to God for the great deliverance here recorded. Every time that, in reading the book, he pronounces the name of Haman, the Jews stamp with their feet, and cry out, "Let the memory of the wicked perish;" and the little children, with wooden hammers provided for the occasion, strike loudly on the walls or seats. They also read from the book of Exodus that passage which records the first battle fought by their ancestors with the Amalekites. It is regarded as a festival of great joy, and even of merriment; the Jews send presents to each other; and the time is spent in gayety and cheerfulness. They even think it allowable to indulge largely in wine in memory of Esther's banquet. The imperfection of the Jewish Calendar sometimes requires an intercalary month. This is always the month Adar, called by way of distinction Ve-Adar or Second Adar. This occurred every two or three years; and the fourteenth day of the first Adar was called the Little Purim; but none of the ceremonies of this feast were observed upon it.

It is most likely that many of the ceremonies of this feast have been gradually changed and increased since its first establishment. But the appointment of the feast itself dates back to the days of Mordecai and Esther; and we think there are some important and profitable thoughts naturally suggested by its appointment.

The first question is, By what authority was the feast established? Was it of human or Divine appointment?

In reference to this question, we have no direct proof. The feast seems to have been established instrumentally through Esther and Mordecai; but we have no direct declaration that they were divinely authorized to make the appointment. The record is made in a book of Canonical Authority; so ever received by the Jews; so received in the time of Christ and by our Lord himself. In this volume no disapproval is shown of the appointment;

and the Jews have ever regarded it as a solemn festival. These, in brief, are the reasons for supposing that they rightly kept it as of Divine appointment. And when we are told that the decree of Esther "confirmed these matters of Purim, and it was written in the book," we understand it as a record in this inspired roll that the feast was established.

There is a very important principle here involved. Few things tend more to the corruption of religion, than the assumed authority in human hands, to appoint stated days for special religious service, and to require their observance. In the Old Testament times the people of God from the beginning of the world observed the Sabbath day, which was appointed at the Creation, and even kept by our first parents in their estate of innocence, and by the children of Israel before they came to Sinai. After they came from Egypt, the Jews observed a number of feasts, of Sabbatical months and Sabbatical years, for one and another purpose, as enjoined by the Mosaic law. The Passover, for example, commemorated the safety of Israel on that dreadful night, when the first born of Egypt were slain; the day of Pentecost was a day of thanksgiving for the first fruits of the harvest; the Sabbatical year and the year of Jubilee (which was a more solemn Sabbatical year twice in a century) were devout recognitions of God's authority and propriety in the land of Canaan, given for their use to his covenant people.

But in the New Testament we find not only a total omission to appoint such days, not only no authority given to any power to establish them, but a direct and absolute freedom asserted from all such observances. The apostle Paul repeatedly speaks of those who esteem one day above another; who observe days and seasons and months and years; and tells us to let no man judge us in respect to new moons or holy-days or sabbaths; for these were but shadows of good things to come. For many and important reasons we do not understand the apostle in these passages as denying the perpetual obligation and Divine authority of the weekly Sabbath. Not only is such an institution imperatively necessary for man's instruction in religious things, and thus absolutely essential to the very existence of the church of God upon earth; not only were there among the Jews several other kinds of Sabbaths of which the apostle speaks, and which might properly be classed with the other festivals he enumerates, as the weekly Sabbath might not be; but there are many other important reasons which show that Paul had no design to invalidate the sanctity of the weekly Sabbath. Not designing, of course, a full discussion of the matter, we suggest these thoughts.

(1.) The weekly Sabbath was not a Jewish ordinance at all; it was ordained at the creation of the world; it was made for man as a race, and not for the Jews as a nation; and as not founded upon the

Jewish law, we ought not to expect it to perish when the Jewish law was abrogated.

(2.) The weekly Sabbath was enjoined in the ten commandments—a dignity conferred upon no Jewish festival. Thus was it evidently designed for a moral precept—permanent like the other parts of that law.

(3.) The entire tenor of the Scriptures enjoins the keeping of the Sabbath day; the apostle Paul himself kept it; and the sacred meetings of the church were held on the first day of the week.

(4.) The Sabbath has actually been kept in the Christian church in all periods of her history, and in all the lands of her wide dispersion. The convincing and indisputable proof that the Jewish new moons, feasts, and fasts were not designed to be permanent in the Christian church, is the fact that they have disappeared for centuries—indeed ever since the apostolic days. If God had designed his people to keep them, he would have given them directions accordingly in his word, and support in his providence. It is a clear proof that the Sabbath was to remain after these other days had been forgotten, that the Sabbath has actually been kept. Is it not perfectly plain, if Paul's language had succeeded in destroying the reverence in the church for the new moons and the weekly Sabbaths alike, that at no subsequent period, in opposition to his inspired authority, could the Sabbath have been revived and re-established? It cannot be possible, that the church of his own age or of any subsequent age, understood Paul to argue against the permanence and obligation of the weekly Sabbath.

But the Apostle did mean to teach, and the history of the church proves that he was understood to mean, that the solemn days of the old economy were not binding upon Christians. The New Testament gives no authority to any man or set of men to appoint solemn days as stated occasions in the worship of God. Such days have indeed been appointed at various times by the authority of church rulers; but the earliest date is far this side of Apostolic authority. And the entire tendency of such human appointments is to impair the sanctity of the Sabbath, to elevate the human ordinance above the Divine, and to make religious services formal. It is no difficult thing to discern that in the Church of Rome her solemn festivals are more sacredly and strictly kept than the Sabbath itself. Indeed the sanctity of the Lord's holy day is destroyed by the festivals of the church. It is difficult, if not impossible, to decide how far such appointments are valid, unless we utterly deny that any authority, short of inspired men, can appoint any stated occasion of religious worship. This remark applies only to stated days of regular occurrence. So in the Directory for Worship of the Presbyterian church, (chapter xiv. § 1, 2,) we have these words: "There is no day under the gospel commanded to be kept holy, except the Lord's day, which is the Christian Sabbath. Nevertheless to observe days of fasting and thanksgiving, as the extraordinary dispensations of Divine providence may direct, we judge both scriptural and rational." Every attempt to multiply religious days, beyond the Divine appointment of the Sabbath, tends to weaken the authority and sanctity of the day divinely appointed; and certain it is, that those Christians, who hallow only the Sabbath, are the most devout and exemplary in keeping the Lord's day.

But passing from this point, let us notice a second inquiry of some interest in connection with this feast established in the days of Esther. How far do such institutions establish the historical truth of the occurrences they are designed to commemorate? Could such a feast possibly be established in memory of certain events—could it be kept by successive generations of a widely scattered people—without any foundation in truth? Or is the history not proved by the existence and influence of the institution?

There are many ways in which human history may be transmitted from one age to another, for a long series of centuries. The simplest undoubtedly is, that children learn from their parents, and pass down the tradition indefinitely. But in these oral methods of communication too much of truth is lost, too much of fable is added, to allow us to place much dependence on the historical relations of the barbarous ages and tribes, to which this method of communication alone is known.

Another method of transmitting history is by written books. But as the writers have not always recorded their personal observations, nor even written concerning their own times; as fictitious histories have been written, and genuine histories altered; and as other matters arise to diminish our confidence in ancient writings, so it is needful that we carefully examine the proofs of genuineness and truthfulness of even written histories.

Another method of transmitting the occurrences of history to subsequent times, is by the erection of some perpetuating structure. For example, the American people have built a monument in memory of the battle of Bunker's Hill. The object of the building is well understood; it is so large that it could not have been put up in a private manner without a full understanding over the country, of its design; the erection took place, not immediately after the battle, but while some of the men were still living who took part in the conflict; and a record is made upon the structure and in our national annals, of the transaction. Does it not seem quite impossible that future ages should doubt that such a battle was fought? Yet such monuments might stand, like the pyramids in Egypt, long after the memory had faded of the events and times with which they were connected. But it will certainly be something wonderful, if the records long illegible upon the ruins of antiquity, shall again be deciphered by human industry; and the world learn that the evidences of human history can be made almost imperishable.

But there is another method by which a true history may be perpetuated and ratified; one which seems to place the entire facts beyond the possibility of forgery or corruption. This is to combine a record written at the time, with such an observance by the people, as shall keep it before their minds, make them familiar with it, and give them a constant interest in it.

For example, on the fourth day of July, A. D. 1776, a paper was presented to an Assembly of Delegates from thirteen States on the American continent in General Congress met; that paper was adopted, the effect being to make them a free people; and that paper spread far and wide among the thousands of their constituents to be handed down to millions of their successors as the Declaration of Independence. But that paper did not go forth alone. The fourth day of July, on which it was signed, became, by common consent, a national jubilee, to be celebrated at each annual return by demonstrations of general joy; and among these, the public reading of the Declaration itself in the ears of all the people. Now make a supposition. Suppose this Union should exist for a thousand years; should fill this Northern continent with powerful States; and should swell its population to as many millions as we now have thousands. Suppose at the end of a thousand years, some historical sceptic should doubt whether such a Declaration was ever made, or that the United States ever became free by such a struggle. Would it not be perfectly just to call upon such a man to account for the enthusiastic national festival on the fourth of July; and for the high regard paid by the entire people to this written paper? If he should allege that the paper was a forgery, then let him explain how such a forgery could possibly be imposed upon a whole people. The whole matter as it exists now, and will exist for ages, is perfectly plain and simple, if that event really took place in Philadelphia in 1776: every body could understand it; and every man, woman, and child felt the influence of it; there was no room for imposition, for the Declaration was publicly spread abroad from that very day. On the other hand, no one can possibly explain how the nation could be led to entertain such a belief without good reason and at a later time. Should any one allege that the Declaration had afterwards been altered, we affirm that by no possibility could a written, and published, and cherished document like that, be altered in a single sentiment. Read by every intelligent man; and every year read publicly aloud in a thousand gatherings in the ears of admiring listeners, it could not be changed. Nor could an intelligent and great nation, like this, be induced to establish such a festival as the fourth of

July, if the great and glorious event it was designed to keep in memory, never actually occurred at all. In point of fact, a double monument like this, consisting of a carefully written document, and of an annual festival held to commemorate what that paper sets forth, is the most enduring monument that man can erect; the most incapable of destruction, on the one hand, or of fraud or corruption, upon the other. Such a monument to prove an important historical truth, becomes even stronger by the lapse of ages and by the wide scattering of those that keep it up. And many generations hence, if the fourth of July should be observed, and the Declaration of our Independence read, by men who reside in such distant cities as Boston, Detroit, Charleston, New Orleans, San Francisco, and Honolulu, every mind must join to say, that such a thing can be explained only by the simplest of all solutions—that the historical event they commemorate did actually occur. All the intervening history would corroborate the proof. The gradual growth and dispersion of the nation over so wide a territory; even the dissensions of the people, leaving untouched these matters of common belief; the references to the Declaration and its results in other histories; its influence upon other nations; and the pride felt by the nation in recounting the past events of their history, and this among the chief; all these things would continue to make imposture in such a case an impossible thing, and to give strength rather than weakness to the evidence with advancing years. The most permanent and satisfactory of human monuments are not built of stone or brass. Like the pyramids of Egypt, these may rise before the gaze of ages that know nothing of their builders. A monument erected in the hearts of a people; a monument on which no false inscription can be written; accompanied by a truthful record of its institution, and kept in memory by a festival, recurring regularly and cheerfully observed, is one which can scarcely be perverted from its original form; and which, taken with the document, is complete evidence of any historical fact.

Now what we here apply to the fourth of July and the Declaration of Independence, may properly and forcibly be applied to the Jewish feast of Purim and the Book of Esther. These two are as intimately connected together as the other two. The Jewish feast has been kept for over two thousand years; and, as we have already noticed, the entire book of Esther is read at its annual celebrations. That there are Apocryphal additions to the book of Esther, is no invalidation of the argument, since these have never been received by the Jews. That this feast did not originate in Jerusalem, the usual ecclesiastical capital of the nation, but that its observance began in the empire of Persia, rather renders the proof stronger than weaker. It could not have spread throughout the wide dispersion from such a beginning; it could not have led the entire

Jewish people to receive the book of Esther among their sacred books, or to observe the Feast of Purim among their sacred festivals, unless good and sufficient reasons had urged them so to do. Knowing, as we do, the dispositions of men, and especially the jealousy of the Jewish people respecting their sacred customs and their religious books, we cannot believe that any reasons, short of the full truth of this narrative, would lead them to receive these things.

Here is a people more widely scattered than any other people; no people more jealous than they of their religious doctrines and their sacred books; no people as a mass and for generations together having superior intelligence; and none better instructed in their own sacred writings. This people all keep the Feast of Purim, and read upon it the book of Esther; their fathers for ages have done so; their national writers, stretching back two thousand years, own the truth, and refer to it in different ways; these things constitute a net-work of complicated circumstantial evidence, impossible to be counterfeited, and more conclusive in the certainty of its proof than any array of positive witnesses could be in such a case.

An eminent scientific gentleman, of whose researches and attainments and standing the American people may well be proud,* tells us that there is a river running through the Atlantic ocean; rising

* Lieut. Maury. "Physical Geography," chap. i.

in the Gulf of Mexico and emptying into the Arctic Seas; its bottom and precipitous banks formed of cold water on either side; its stream, the heated water of the Torrid Zone; its current swifter, and its volume of water a thousand times beyond the Mississippi or the Amazon; and spreading as it proceeds northward, it tempers the climate of Western Europe and clothes its shores with a delightful verdure, that widely contrasts with the same latitude on the other side of the ocean. The effects of this stream were felt for the good of western Europe long before its existence was known, or philosophy had investigated its causes, and had taught us to admire in it the wisdom of God's providence; and among the causes which led to the discovery of this Western Continent, we must number the drifts carried across the ocean by this remarkable river. The brother-in-law of Columbus found, in the Atlantic, west of the Madeira Islands, a curiously carved piece of timber that had floated from the west;* trees torn up by the roots had come in the same direction; and the bodies of two men, with features different from any known upon the Eastern Continent were cast upon the coast of the Azores.

The Scriptures, in the bold figure of oriental diction, liken the nations of men to "many waters;" and through the vast ocean of human population that has tossed its restless waves around our globe for 3500 years past, there runs a remarkable river;

---

* Robertson's America, p. 44. Irving's Columbus, p. 21.

its source is in the plains of Mesopotamia; its volume is vast beyond any other living stream that can be attributed to one national origin; unlike the Atlantic river, it has spread all over the world, still as distinctly dividing its waters from those in immediate contact with it.

The maintenance of the Jewish national existence, while they have for ages been scattered among other nations and yet have been perfectly distinct from them, is as strange a thing as a river running through the ocean, and refusing to mingle with the surrounding mass of waters; and as this great current in the Atlantic has important uses in God's providence, so this distinct current in the ocean of humanity has its important design in the orderings of God's moral government. Other nations have been deprived of their liberties and scattered from their homes; but a few generations sufficed in each case to lose and absorb them in the surrounding population. Upon this continent now a great experiment is going on, of many nations losing their national distinctions in one; and with the third generation, we can scarcely distinguish a trace of the distinctive European origin. But, not stopping now to consider the single and strange exception of the gipsy race, no people has ever existed like the Jews, maintaining their unbroken national existence and their uncorrupted national books for so many generations, and through such violent changes. Upon this stream in the ocean of time, and from another stream branching off from it in the form of Christianity, two thousand years ago, have floated down to us the most important teachings and institutions which the God of providence and grace would establish and maintain among the sons of men. A man might just as well affirm that the Gulf Stream, with all its beneficent influences, was the contrivance of human wit, as attempt to class among the follies of human imposture, the proof of historical verity afforded by the incontrovertible truths of the Jewish nationality. Past ages have not discerned, much less designed, the plans of Divine wisdom to govern the physical and the moral world. We can hardly decide which is the more remarkable: the teachings themselves, or the historical proof of their truth. The nations to whom have been borne the institutions and the instructions which this Providential stream carries along with it, exhibit an elevation of intellectual and moral character quite as striking as the physical differences between the Emerald Isle in the Gulf Stream, and the frozen coasts of Labrador, which are out of the Gulf Stream, and yet are in the same latitude with Ireland. Let it be our wisdom to note these contrasts in God's moral, as well as his physical rule; and to ascribe them to their just cause; the wisdom of Him who made and governs the world.

If any man should attempt to construct an argument to prove the truth of any ancient records, he cannot even imagine one more natural than this; it is quite impossible to find one more conclusive; and not one historical document out of a thousand has proof of its verity in anywise comparable to such as this. And when we reflect that the same kind of an argument and with peculiar conclusiveness of reasoning in each case can be adopted for at least three things in the Bible: that there are three double monuments—a book and a positive institution—erected by Divine wisdom and perpetuated among men together; we may understand in some degree how remarkably the historical proofs of the Bible preponderate over all other evidences of human history. We have no institutions handed down from antiquity in so direct a line, and accompanied by the written explanation of their founders. When Moses wrote the first historical books of the Bible, he taught the Jewish people to observe the feast of the Passover; when Mordecai wrote the last historical book of the Old Testament, the feast of Purim was established; when Christ and his apostles gave the church the New Testament, the Lord's supper was ordained. These three feasts are yet kept by Jews and Christians; and it is impossible to give a satisfactory account of their existence and wide adoption, without acknowledging in full the authenticity of the volume which gives them all their authority. The doctrinal differences in Christian churches respecting the Lord's supper only strengthen the argument; since no differences exist respecting the history of its institution, and all agree in referring to the same written document. It seems impossible to give greater historical evidence to any book, than God has gathered around the Bible. The sacred volume has all the evidence in its favour that any ancient history has; and superadded, it has proofs that belong to no ancient author. It may indeed be questioned, whether a continued evidence from miracles would be of more force to convince men of the truth of the Bible, than this perfect and adamantine chain of circumstantial historical proof to the mind that candidly and intelligently weighs it.

And now, after these long reflections, we may return again for a few moments to the narrative of the book of Esther. As the chronicles of the kings of Media and Persia have perished, for they had no monument erected in the hearts of a perpetual people to keep them in remembrance; we have no knowledge from other sources of the tribute laid by king Ahasuerus upon the land, and upon the islands. Possibly among the wonders of modern researches into the remains of antiquity, we may yet reckon some proofs corroborative of the book of Esther; as indeed flying rumour repeated a little while ago that the tesselated marble pavement of the palace of Shushan had been disinterred; and even the names and deeds of Mordecai and Esther had been read upon newly discovered monuments. However this may be, ancient historians tell us that the kings of Persia, reigning before the time of

Alexander the Great, exacted tokens of submission from the surrounding lands; but of any special tax like that here referred to, or of the greatness of Mordecai the Jew, we know only what is here told us. It is gratifying to be informed that in his prosperity Mordecai maintained the same inflexible integrity that had characterized his earlier days. He still sought the prosperity of his people, and spoke peace to all his seed. None are better prepared for prosperity than those that have well endured trial. And thus we see that the God of Jacob gave his people his protection in the land of their exile.

After the death of Mordecai and during the subsequent troubles of the Persian empire, and after its overthrow by Alexander the Great, the Jews suffered many evils; both those in Persia, and those that had returned to Palestine. It does not belong to the present lectures to consider these matters. As before intimated they were all preparatory to the coming of Christ, and the spread of the gospel was facilitated by these revolutions, and the wide dispersion of the Jewish exiles.

Here then closes the narrative of the book. Our curiosity craves more; and perhaps to gratify this craving, the apocryphal chapters were written. But besides the refutation we have already given to their claims, we may add that the last chapter enjoins the Persians upon their peril to keep this festival. We have no evidence that they ever did so; and the remarkable historical proof already referred to, totally fails to support the apocryphal additions.

In concluding the lectures on this book, we may indulge a few reflections:

1. Let us learn the great value of the Old Testament records. They were written by holy men for no trifling or transient purpose; but for the permanent instruction of the church of God. Christians would take a deeper interest in them, if they studied them more closely. This book of God, like all his works, will bear close investigation. No man knows how much study any subject will bear, until he gives it his serious attention. Unwise as well as irreverent are they who neglect the Old Testament. It has claims on our regard founded upon the same Divine authorship with the New. In the later books we have more advanced principles and clearer revelations; but the two are one system of religious truth. The Old cannot be properly read without the light of the New: nor can the New be fully comprehended without the study of the Old. The lessons of the Old should much engage our thoughts. The saints of former times belonged to the same church with ourselves; and the trials and triumphs of their faith should support and encourage us in conflicts that are substantially the same.

2. We have seen in these lectures the finger of God in providence, specially as caring for and preserving his church. And our wonder is called forth by the simplicity of the whole. All the events in

this interesting history, if we may use the language of common life, occur naturally. There is not an incident recorded in the book, that seems forced or strained; the current of events, the emotions and feelings of men, the conjunctions of times and purposes, the influence of motives—are all such as we see in the world around us. There is hardly a single thing of which, taken by itself, apart and separated from its connections, we would say, *this God has done;* and yet there is hardly a single thing taken in its needful connection with all the rest, but we must say of it, *this God has done.* The separate parts of the whole, considered separately, are no more strange for man to do, than a thousand things going on in the world every day; but the working of all these things together, and the result of the whole, are infinitely worthy of the wisdom and power, the justice and grace of God. Now when we look at our own affairs, we look at the separate parts; we see them disjointed; we are not capable of putting them all harmoniously together; and we fail to recognize the wisdom and goodness of Providence because we are incompetent to discover his definite designs.

An ancient humorist tells a story of a foolish fellow who had a house to sell; and carried around with him a brick, as a specimen. We can judge of Providence by single incidents about as wisely as we can judge of a mansion from one portion of its materials. Can any man decide what are the figures, or what the beauty of an exquisite carpet, by seeing a sample of the wool from which it is woven? Let us not be guilty of the folly of prejudging God's providence. The events around us and in which we are taking part, may apparently be the materials of but a common web; but the Workman is one of infinite skill; and it is beyond our penetration to judge what he will make out of it. The hearing of a sermon, or the reading of a book, may be the turning point under his blessing and direction for infinite issues. We may be assured of this, that faith in God's truth shall never be confounded. As in the days of Esther, so now, "all things work together for good to those that love God." "All things" are not intrinsically right; some things are evil, and naturally tend only to evil; but "working together," the result is good. In some complicated machinery, we very often see one movement horizontal and another oblique, one wheel turning in one direction, and another the reverse, yet the result of the whole is some harmonious and beneficial result; so in Providence, the end shows Divine wisdom. As in the Book of Esther, we see wicked men forming their plans and urging forward their purposes; and righteous men praying and weeping and hoping and labouring; and God over all, controlling both, restraining the evil, and blessing his people; so is it now; so will it ever be in the world. The present is for us the time of duty and responsibility; hereafter we shall see the results and recognize God's wisdom in Providence.

3. If earthly dignity and honours in their best estate are vanity, let the humility and faith, the zeal and holiness of Esther and Mordecai teach us the true path of glory and honour and immortality. Here is a way of discharging the pressing duties of life, and securing in them the favour of God and the unfading honours of a kingdom that cannot be moved. As sinful men, the first requisite to citizenship in the heavenly kingdom, is to be reconciled to God; to be submissive to his Spirit's guidance; and dependent on the atoning merits of his Son. Let each soul ponder the wickedness and the danger of rebellion against God. Let the wicked forsake a way that must end in destruction; and the unrighteous man the thoughts that must end in shame. With humble, but with sincere and believing hearts let us draw near to that God, who invites our confidence and encourages our hopes. If any one, in any situation of life, and for any reason supposes that he can presume upon safety, though he timidly shrinks back from the plain path of duty, he has failed to learn a most important lesson which the book of Esther should have taught us. The duty of each moment and of each station, done at the proper time and by the proper person, with a wise union of earnest labour and of entire dependence upon God, is an important truth again and again urged upon us in these brief chapters.

www.ingramcontent.com/pod-product-compliance
Lightning Source LLC
LaVergne TN
LVHW010230110826
845151LV00004B/1254

9781425525606